"This series is a tremendous resource for those wanting to study and teach the Bible with an understanding of how the gospel is woven throughout Scripture. Here are gospel-minded pastors and scholars doing gospel business from all the Scriptures. This is a biblical and theological feast preparing God's people to apply the entire Bible to all of life with heart and mind wholly committed to Christ's priorities."

> **BRYAN CHAPELL,** President Emeritus, Covenant Theological Seminary; Senior Pastor, Grace Presbyterian Church, Peoria, Illinois

"Mark Twain may have smiled when he wrote to a friend, 'I didn't have time to write you a short letter, so I wrote you a long letter.' But the truth of Twain's remark remains serious and universal, because well-reasoned, compact writing requires extra time and extra hard work. And this is what we have in the Crossway Bible study series *Knowing the Bible*. The skilled authors and notable editors provide the contours of each book of the Bible as well as the grand theological themes that bind them together as one Book. Here, in a 12-week format, are carefully wrought studies that will ignite the mind and the heart."

> **R. KENT HUGHES,** Visiting Professor of Practical Theology, Westminster Theological Seminary

"*Knowing the Bible* brings together a gifted team of Bible teachers to produce a high-quality series of study guides. The coordinated focus of these materials is unique: biblical content, provocative questions, systematic theology, practical application, and the gospel story of God's grace presented all the way through Scripture."

> **PHILIP G. RYKEN,** President, Wheaton College

"These *Knowing the Bible* volumes provide a significant and very welcome variation on the general run of inductive Bible studies. This series provides substantial instruction, as well as teaching through the very questions that are asked. *Knowing the Bible* then goes even further by showing how any given text links with the gospel, the whole Bible, and the formation of theology. I heartily endorse this orientation of individual books to the whole Bible and the gospel, and I applaud the demonstration that sound theology was not something invented later by Christians, but is right there in the pages of Scripture."

> **GRAEME L. GOLDSWORTHY,** former lecturer, Moore Theological College; author, *According to Plan, Gospel and Kingdom, The Gospel in Revelation*, and *Gospel and Wisdom*

"What a gift to earnest, Bible-loving, Bible-searching believers! The organization and structure of the Bible study format presented through the *Knowing the Bible* series is so well conceived. Students of the Word are led to understand the content of passages through perceptive, guided questions, and they are given rich insights and application all along the way in the brief but illuminating sections that conclude each study. What potential growth in depth and breadth of understanding these studies offer! One can only pray that vast numbers of believers will discover more of God and the beauty of his Word through these rich studies."

> **BRUCE A. WARE,** Professor of Christian Theology, The Southern Baptist Theological Seminary

KNOWING THE BIBLE

J. I. Packer, Theological Editor
Dane C. Ortlund, Series Editor
Lane T. Dennis, Executive Editor

. . . . . .

Genesis	Psalms	Jonah, Micah, and Nahum	Ephesians
Exodus	Proverbs		Philippians
Leviticus	Ecclesiastes	Haggai, Zechariah, and Malachi	Colossians and Philemon
Numbers	Song of Solomon		
Deuteronomy	Isaiah	Matthew	1–2 Thessalonians
Joshua	Jeremiah	Mark	1–2 Timothy and Titus
Judges	Lamentations, Habakkuk, and Zephaniah	Luke	
Ruth and Esther		John	Hebrews
1–2 Samuel	Ezekiel	Acts	James
1–2 Kings	Daniel	Romans	1–2 Peter and Jude
1–2 Chronicles	Hosea	1 Corinthians	1–3 John
Ezra and Nehemiah	Joel, Amos, and Obadiah	2 Corinthians	Revelation
Job		Galatians	

. . . . . .

J. I. PACKER is the former Board of Governors' Professor of Theology at Regent College (Vancouver, BC). Dr. Packer earned his DPhil at the University of Oxford. He is known and loved worldwide as the author of the best-selling book *Knowing God*, as well as many other titles on theology and the Christian life. He serves as the General Editor of the ESV Bible and as the Theological Editor for the *ESV Study Bible*.

LANE T. DENNIS is CEO of Crossway, a not-for-profit publishing ministry. Dr. Dennis earned his PhD from Northwestern University. He is Chair of the ESV Bible Translation Oversight Committee and Executive Editor of the *ESV Study Bible*.

DANE C. ORTLUND is Chief Publishing Officer at Crossway. He is a graduate of Covenant Theological Seminary (MDiv, ThM) and Wheaton College (BA, PhD). Dr. Ortlund has authored several books and scholarly articles in the areas of Bible, theology, and Christian living.

ROMANS

A 12-WEEK STUDY

Jared C. Wilson

::CROSSWAY®

WHEATON, ILLINOIS

Cover design: Simplicated Studio

First printing 2013

Printed in the United States of America

All emphases in Scripture quotations have been added by the author.

Trade paperback ISBN: 978-1-4335-3441-6
PDF ISBN: 978-1-4335-3442-3
Mobipocket ISBN: 978-1-4335-3443-0
EPub ISBN: 978-1-4335-3444-7

Crossway is a publishing ministry of Good News Publishers.

VP			30	29	28	27	26	25	24	23	22	21	20
22	21	20	19	18	17	16	15	14	13	12	11	10	

TABLE OF CONTENTS

SERIES PREFACE

KNOWING THE BIBLE, as the series title indicates, was created to help readers know and understand the meaning, the message, and the God of the Bible. Each volume in the series consists of 12 units that progressively take the reader through a clear, concise study of that book of the Bible. In this way, any given volume can fruitfully be used in a 12-week format either in group study, such as in a church-based context, or in individual study. Of course, these 12 studies could be completed in fewer or more than 12 weeks, as convenient, depending on the context in which they are used.

Each study unit gives an overview of the text at hand before digging into it with a series of questions for reflection or discussion. The unit then concludes by highlighting the gospel of grace in each passage ("Gospel Glimpses"), identifying whole-Bible themes that occur in the passage ("Whole-Bible Connections"), and pinpointing Christian doctrines that are affirmed in the passage ("Theological Soundings").

The final component to each unit is a section for reflecting on personal and practical implications from the passage at hand. The layout provides space for recording responses to the questions proposed, and we think readers need to do this to get the full benefit of the exercise. The series also includes definitions of key words. These definitions are indicated by a note number in the text and are found at the end of each chapter.

Lastly, to help understand the Bible in this deeper way, we urge readers to use the ESV Bible and the *ESV Study Bible*, which are available in various print and digital formats, including online editions at esv.org. The Knowing the Bible series is also available online.

May the Lord greatly bless your study as you seek to know him through knowing his Word.

J. I. Packer
Lane T. Dennis

Week 1: Overview

Getting Acquainted

The apostle Paul's letter to the Romans is the longest of his letters and is brimming with his exhilarating captivation with the gospel of Jesus Christ. Romans can be seen as an epic in one sense, not just because of its length but because of its breadth and sweep. Paul begins his instruction with words about creation and the natural order, and then proceeds to show how mankind's disobedience brought disruption to them. Then Paul moves methodically—but beautifully—through the story of the Bible itself, recounting God's justice and grace throughout history, from the days of the patriarchs until the time of his writing. At the same time, Paul lays out the "anatomy" of salvation, telling both the wide-lens story of God's work in history to restore fallen creation and the finer, narrow-lens story of how God saves sinners through the life, death, and resurrection of his Son Jesus Christ. Readers of Romans see both the wide-angle view and the close-up view of salvation.

All of this is even more remarkable when we consider that Paul probably wrote this letter in response to specific doctrinal and practical questions. How does law relate to faith? How do we as Christians relate to the pre-Christian era? How were those who came before Christ saved? How does gospel ministry to the Gentiles affect the Jews' standing with God? What unifies Jews and Gentiles in Christian practice? What divides them?

Paul's letter to the Romans sounds many minor notes (which does not mean they are insignificant) but every note serves to create the symphony revealing God's righteousness[1] brought to bear in history through the saving work of Jesus. The major theme throughout this masterpiece is the powerful message of the cross of Christ, where God's wrath for sin and mercy on sinners finds its fulfillment and unity.

Placing It in the Larger Story

While Romans is not the earliest of Paul's epistles (letters) to appear in the canon of Scripture (1 and 2 Thessalonians, 1 and 2 Corinthians, and Galatians were probably written earlier) it serves as a foundation of sorts for all his other letters. This is one reason, in addition to its length, why it appears first in the canon's epistles. The major ideas of all of Paul's other letters—sin, Christ, and the gospel—find their fullest expression in Romans, even though there are some major ideas explored in the shorter letters which are not explored in Romans (doctrines of the church, the nature of Christ, the end times, etc.).

The letter of Romans serves as a grand theological blueprint for the gospel doctrine undergirding the rest of the New Testament. This includes the letters of Peter and the letter of James, who at first glance may appear to diverge from Paul's teaching on justification.[2] Appearing in the New Testament immediately after the four Gospels and Acts, Paul's letter to the Romans unpacks the significance of who Jesus is and what he did. Paul takes the Gospel narratives of Jesus and his apostles—as well as the Old Testament revelation they fulfilled—and reveals their doctrinal implications. In other words, Paul explains the theological meaning of the overarching story stretching from Genesis to Jesus and beyond, into the future.

Key Passage

"For all have sinned and fall short of the glory of God, and are justified by his grace as a gift, through the redemption that is in Christ Jesus, whom God put forward as a propitiation by his blood, to be received by faith." (Rom. 3:23–25)

Date and Historical Background

Paul most likely wrote his letter to the Romans in AD 57, while on his third missionary journey (see Acts 20:2–3), probably while in Corinth. Notes left by copyists at the end of two early manuscripts identify Corinth as its place of composition. Also, both Phoebe (Rom. 16:1–2) and Gaius (v. 23) had connections to Corinth.

The epistle to the Romans is one of at least two letters Paul wrote to a church he had not visited or founded. Perhaps the church had been founded by inhabitants of Rome who had been in Jerusalem at Pentecost in Acts 2, had become believers, and had then returned to Rome (see Acts 2:10).

The circumstances giving rise to the letter are not entirely clear, but it seems that Paul was addressing theological questions that had been posed to him. One main cause for these questions was simmering hostility between Jewish and Gentile believers in the Roman church. Paul intended to visit Rome (Rom. 1:11–13), and this letter was meant to serve as an introduction to his teaching. Paul also hoped his letter would give rise to a broader missionary operation with Rome as its home base.

At the time of Paul's writing, Nero was emperor. Rome was not just the base of the Roman empire but was considered the base of civilization itself. It is no wonder that Paul hoped to see his readers' world turned upside down for the sake of God's kingdom.[3] Politics and paganism freely merged in the capital city. In its day, Rome was New York, Los Angeles, London, and Paris rolled into one. But in every way the claims of Paul's gospel transcended those of imperial Rome.

Outline

I. The Gospel as the Revelation of the Righteousness of God (1:1–17)

II. God's Righteousness in His Wrath against Sinners (1:18–3:20)

III. The Saving Righteousness of God (3:21–4:25)

IV. Hope as a Result of Righteousness by Faith (5:1–8:39)

V. God's Righteousness Extended to Israel and to the Gentiles (9:1–11:36)

VI. God's Righteousness in Everyday Life (12:1–15:13)

VII. The Extension of God's Righteousness through the Pauline Mission (15:14–16:23)

VIII. Final Summary of the Gospel of the Righteousness of God (16:25–27)

As You Get Started . . .

What is your general understanding of the role of Paul's letter to the Romans? What do you think this letter uniquely contributes?

How do you understand the contribution of Romans to Christian theology? From your current knowledge of Romans, what does Paul teach us about God, humanity, sin, redemption, and other doctrines?

Some of Christianity's more "famous" Bible verses come from the book of Romans. Which ones are you familiar with?

Romans contains some of the more provocative teachings of the Bible as well. Paul teaches on election and predestination, for instance, as well as the way of salvation for the Jewish people and his plan for Israel in the future. What perplexes you about Romans? Are there any confusing parts to this letter that you would like to resolve as you begin this study?

> ## As You Finish This Unit . . .

Take a moment to ask for the Lord's blessing and help as you engage in this study of Romans.

Definitions

[1] **Righteousness** – The quality of being morally right and without sin; one of God's distinctive attributes. God imputes righteousness to (i.e., justifies) those who trust in Jesus Christ.

[2] **Justification** – The act of God's grace in declaring sinners fully acquitted and counting them as righteous before him on the basis of the finished work of Christ, received through faith alone.

[3] **Kingdom of God** – The rule of God manifested in the long-awaited restoration of his people and indeed the whole world. When Jesus came two thousand years ago, he announced that the kingdom of God had arrived (Mark 1:15; Luke 17:20–21). Yet because of ongoing rebellion and rejection of Jesus and his rule, the kingdom still awaits its final consummation and fulfillment in Jesus' second coming (Mark 14:25). For this reason we pray for the kingdom to come (Matt. 6:10).

WEEK 2: THE GOSPEL AS THE REVELATION OF THE RIGHTEOUSNESS OF GOD

Romans 1:1–17

The Place of the Passage

This opening passage to Paul's letter sets the stage for all that comes after. In his customary style, a mix of theological richness and passionate self-disclosure, Paul incorporates the flavor of worship even in the way he greets the Roman church. He appears always to be exulting in the truth and power of the gospel.[1] He even manages to give a soaring summary of the good news between his identification of himself (1:1) and his addressing of his recipients (1:7). The description of the gospel in 1:16–17 then serves as the theme statement for the whole letter.

The Big Picture

In Romans 1:1–17, Paul expresses his desire to come to Rome and gives a stirring description of the power of the gospel.

> ## Reflection and Discussion

Read through the complete passage for this study, Romans 1:1–17. Then review the shorter passages below and write your own notes on the following questions. (For further background, see the *ESV Study Bible*, pages 2157–2158; also available online at esv.org.)

1. A Gospel Greeting (1:1–7)

In 1:2–3, Paul references the Old Testament and its promise of Jesus. Jesus himself explained that he was the culmination of the whole Old Testament (Luke 24:25–27, 44–47; see also John 5:39–47). What are some Old Testament passages you can think of that promise or anticipate the coming of Christ?

Paul speaks of "the obedience of faith" in 1:5 (note also 10:16; 16:26). Most Christians are accustomed to speaking of faith and obedience as completely separate categories, and for very good biblical reason. What might Paul mean by "the obedience of faith"?

Paul is writing to the church in Rome in part to strategically carry out his desire to spread Christ's name among all the nations (1:5). From what else you know about Paul and this specific letter, what are some other evidences of this desire of Paul's?

2. Paul's Gospel Obligations (1:8–15)

When we trust in Jesus Christ for the forgiveness of our sins, being justified[2] by God's grace in Christ received through faith, we are set free from the obligations of the law for justification. At the same time, we are set free *to* the obligations of the law for witness to God's faithfulness. In other words, we are saved, not *by* good works but *for* them (Matt. 5:16; Eph. 2:10). What does Paul feel obligated to do "first" (Rom. 1:8)? How does this first impulse of his reflect the message of the good news?

Paul is never shy about sharing his feelings in his letters. But the feelings he expresses—whether joy or sadness or even anger—are always shaped by his ultimate desire. According to 1:11–15, what are some reasons he longs to visit Rome, and what is his ultimate desire?

Why would Paul, a Jew, believe he is "under obligation" to Greeks and barbarians (1:14)?

Reviewing 1:8–14, why does Paul say in 1:15 that he is eager to preach the gospel to the Romans?

3. The Righteous Shall Live by Faith (1:16–17)

Why is Paul "not ashamed of the gospel" (1:16)? How does this answer under-cut shame, practically speaking?

How is the "righteousness of God" revealed in the gospel (1:17)?

Read through the following three sections on *Gospel Glimpses, Whole-Bible Connections*, and *Theological Soundings*. Then take time to reflect on the *Personal Implications* these sections may have for your walk with the Lord.

Gospel Glimpses

THE GOSPEL CENTER. We see in this opening greeting from Paul to the church in Rome how the good news of Jesus functions as the centerpiece for the Christian's devotional life and evangelistic mission. In the very beginning, Paul says he is "set apart *for* the gospel" (Rom. 1:1), reinforcing what he has claimed elsewhere, that the gospel is "of first importance" (1 Cor. 15:3). All of Paul's life and ministry flows from this blessed fixation: Jesus Christ crucified, dead, and raised to glory. So for Paul in Romans and elsewhere, the first obedience is the "obedience of faith" (Rom. 1:5). In other words, the first imperative (the thing to *do*) is to focus on the indicative (the thing that *is*) and then respond accordingly. By asserting the centrality of the gospel, Paul is really just asserting the centrality of Jesus Christ himself. It is "through Jesus Christ" that he is able to offer thanksgiving to God (Rom. 1:8), for instance.

THE GOSPEL'S POWER. In Romans 1:9, Paul says that he serves with his spirit "in the gospel." He is implying here what he says explicitly elsewhere: the gospel is not just the power for salvation at conversion but the power that sustains the whole of the Christian life, "from faith for faith" (1:17). Paul did not view the gospel as something beyond which mature Christians graduate. Rather, the gospel is the very power that drives the maturing process, which is lifelong.

GRACE TO YOU. Paul's customary greeting is "grace to you" (Rom. 1:7). Paul knows that "faith comes from hearing" (10:17), and so as he is writing these sacred words breathed out by God, he is reminding believers who God is—as Peter puts it, "the God of all grace" (1 Pet. 5:10). In short, when Paul writes "grace to you" at the start of his letters, he is indicating that the preeminent message he brings is one of grace. This is why Paul then closes his letters with the words "grace be *with* you." Paul knows that the word of God's gospel is powerful, bringing the irresistible call of salvation to those who belong to God and supplying the strength of our faithful God to sustain them all the way to their glorification,[3] so he confidently bookends his letters with "grace to you" and "grace . . . with you" (Rom. 16:20).

Whole-Bible Connections

SON OF GOD. In Romans 1:4 Jesus is "declared to be [that is, disclosed as] the Son of God" through his resurrection from the dead. While the title "Son of God" is sometimes used (especially in John's Gospel) simply to refer to Christ's deity, the title here brings to fruition the Old Testament expectation of the son of God to come. In Luke 3:38 we learn that Adam was "the son of God." But we know that Jesus is the "true and better" Adam (see Rom. 5:19). The Father even designated Israel as his "firstborn son" (Ex. 4:22). But Jesus becomes the redemption for the failure of that "son" too. Indeed, John 1:12 tells us that it is only through the true Son of God that others can also qualify to be called children of God. Jesus is the true and eternal Son, now incarnate, and those who trust him become children of God by adoption (Rom. 8:15–17). The biblical hope of sonship to the Father reverberates throughout the father-son stories of the Old Testament and echoes into the New Testament parables of fathers and sons (most notably the famous "prodigal son" story). These all find their unity and fulfillment in Jesus Christ, who on the cross was rejected and forsaken by the Father (Matt. 27:46) so that we sinners could be accepted freely by the Father as his own sons and daughters (1 John 3:1).

"FOR THE SAKE OF HIS NAME AMONG ALL THE NATIONS." Paul expresses his missional concern in Romans 1:5. His desire in proclaiming the gospel of Jesus is that God's name would be exalted among all the nations of the world. In doing this, he is participating in God's ancient plan to make a name for himself in all the world. As early as the start of the Abrahamic covenant,[4] God shares his plan that through the nation that comes from Abraham "all the nations of the earth shall be blessed" (Gen. 18:18). In Isaiah 49:6, we learn that Israel is to be "a light for the nations." This prophecy is picked up in Luke 2:32 and Acts 13:47 (and 26:23) and applied to the work of Jesus Christ, in whom there is neither Jew nor Greek, but all are one (Gal. 3:28). Paul's articulation of gospel mission in Romans 1:5 is not an innovation but is in full accord with the grand design of God's saving purposes down through history.

"THE RIGHTEOUS SHALL LIVE BY FAITH." Salvation by grace received through faith, apart from works of the law, is not a New Testament invention. When Paul writes these words in Romans 1:17, he is quoting Habakkuk 2:4 and recalling the way of salvation from the beginning. As Paul will explain more fully in Romans 4, even for Abraham, the father of the Jewish people, it was not obedience but trusting faith that put him right with God (see also Galatians 3). When we exercise faith in Jesus Christ alone for the forgiveness of our sins, resisting the temptation to rely even in part on our own performance, we are "the sons of Abraham" (Gal. 3:7) and are blessed along with him (Gal. 3:9).

Theological Soundings

SON OF GOD. From the perspective of the whole Bible's teaching, to call Jesus God's Son refers both to his positional relationship with the Father (a functional subordination of child to father) and to his relationship of "essence" with the Father (a qualitative equality with the Father). The sonship of Jesus is eternal. He was not adopted by the Father. When the Scriptures say Jesus identifies himself as the Son of God, then, they are not just pointing out that Jesus is in relationship to the Father as a human son is to his father but that Jesus is in relationship to the Father as very God to very God. Even the Pharisees understood this: "This was why the Jews were seeking all the more to kill him, because not only was he breaking the Sabbath, but he was even calling God his own Father, making himself equal with God" (John 5:18; also 10:30). Biblically speaking, calling Jesus the Son of God is calling him God (John 1:1, 18.)

RESURRECTION. Paul refers to Jesus' resurrection from the dead (Rom. 1:4) as authentication of his sonship and lordship. The resurrection of Jesus was bodily; it was not just a temporary resuscitation. He truly died as the result of his crucifixion. He did not faint or swoon. And he truly came back to life (1 Cor. 15:20). At the same time, Jesus' resurrected body was not the same as his pre-crucifixion body. In some ways, to be sure, it was the same, bearing the same wounds, for instance (John 20:27), and maintaining the ability to perform basic bodily actions such as eating (John 21:9–14). But in some significant ways, it was very different. He could pass through locked doors, for instance

(John 20:19), and apparently was not immediately recognizable to some of his closest followers (Luke 24:13–16). Paul elsewhere tells us about the uniqueness of a resurrected body: it is a glorified body (1 Cor. 15:42–47). Jesus' bodily resurrection, which guarantees ours, is the Christian's great hope—without it, we may as well give up the Christian faith (1 Cor. 15:16, 32).

Personal Implications

Take time to reflect on the implications of Romans 1:1–17 for your own life today. Make notes below on the personal implications for your walk with the Lord of (1) the *Gospel Glimpses*, (2) the *Whole-Bible Connections*, (3) the *Theological Soundings*, and (4) this passage as a whole.

1. Gospel Glimpses

2. Whole-Bible Connections

3. Theological Soundings

4. Romans 1:1–17

> ### As You Finish This Unit . . .

Take a moment to ask for the Lord's blessing and help as you continue in this study of Romans. And take a moment also to look back through this unit of study, to reflect on some key things that the Lord may be teaching you.

Definitions

[1] **Gospel** – A common translation for a Greek word meaning "good news," that is, the good news of Jesus Christ and the salvation he made possible by his crucifixion, burial, and resurrection. Gospel with an initial capital letter refers to each of the biblical accounts of Jesus' life on earth (Matthew, Mark, Luke, and John).

[2] **Justification** – The act of God's grace in bringing sinners into a new covenant relationship with himself and counting them as righteous before him through the forgiveness of sins (Rom. 3:20–26).

[3] **Glorification** – The work of God in believers to bring them to the ultimate and perfect stage of salvation—full Christlikeness—following his justification and sanctification of them (Rom. 8:29–30). Glorification includes believers receiving imperishable resurrection bodies at Christ's return (1 Cor. 15:42–43).

[4] **Covenant** – A binding agreement between two parties, typically involving a formal statement of their relationship. This agreement includes a list of stipulations and obligations for both parties, a list of witnesses to the agreement, and a list of curses for unfaithfulness and blessings for faithfulness to the agreement. The OT is more properly understood as the old covenant, meaning the agreement established between God and his people prior to the coming of Jesus Christ to establish the new covenant (NT).

WEEK 3: GOD'S RIGHTEOUSNESS IN HIS WRATH AGAINST SINNERS

Romans 1:18–3:20

The Place of the Passage

Paul has now proclaimed the power of the gospel to save believing sinners, whomever they may be (1:17). He has also asserted in the same breath that this power working through faith has strength enough both to justify once for all time and to sustain Christian living. "The righteous shall live by faith." Now Paul transitions into supporting evidence in service of his assertions. The first place he must go is to the harsh reality of sin and human sinfulness. With masterful skill, Paul in 1:18–3:20 lays bare mankind's falling short of God's glory while maintaining that God's glory remains nevertheless undiminished. He also begins to explore God's righteous wrath toward sin. This sets the stage for Paul's exploration in Romans 3–8 of God's grace in justifying and sanctifying sinners.

The Big Picture

Paul reveals the extent of our disobedience against the righteous God.

19

> ## Reflection and Discussion

Read through the complete passage for this study, Romans 1:18–3:20. Then review the shorter passages below and write your own notes on the following questions. (For further background, see the *ESV Study Bible*, pages 2158–2163; also available online at esv.org.)

1. The Unrighteousness of the Gentiles (1:18–32)

Romans 1:20 is reminiscent of Psalm 19:1—"The heavens declare the glory of God." How do "the things that have been made" give clear evidence of God's "eternal power and divine nature"?

Throughout the passage, Paul uses phrases like "God gave them up in the lusts of their hearts" (1:24), "God gave them up to dishonorable passions" (1:26), and "God gave them up to a debased mind" (1:28). What implications do such proclamations have for the idea of "free will"?

If sinners "suppress the truth" (1:18), how can Paul say that the truth is "clearly perceived" (1:20)?

In this passage, Paul is revealing that even the irreligious—in this case, classified as Gentiles, or "non-Jews"—are aware of a holy standard. What are some ways in which even those who deny God demonstrate a tacit awareness of moral absolutes?

---

2. The Unrighteousness of the Jews (2:1–3:8)

Now Paul begins to focus more narrowly on those inside the religious community. It's not just "those people out there" who are sinners, but "we insiders" too. Why does Paul say that when we judge others, we condemn ourselves (2:1)?

If tribulation will come to every evildoer, first to Jews and then to Greeks (2:9), and peace to everyone who does good, first to Jews and then to Greeks (v. 10), how can Paul say God shows no partiality (v. 11)?

In Romans 2:12–14 Paul *appears* to say that obedience will justify Gentiles. When we interpret any biblical text, we have to keep it in its context. How does 2:15–29 help to clarify what Paul is saying?

21

According to Romans 3:1–2, what advantage do Jews have?

3. The Unrighteousness of All People (3:9–20)

We are accustomed to speaking of unbelievers as "seekers." There is indeed a sense in which all people are seeking God—in the sense that they are seeking to satisfy their need for God with all sorts of things that aren't God. But what does Paul (quoting Ps. 14:1–3) mean when he says "no one seeks for God" (Rom. 3:11)?

How does Romans 3:18 relate to 3:11?

According to Romans 3:20, what might we call the "catch-22"—both the benefit and the detriment—of the works of the law?

Read through the following three sections on *Gospel Glimpses*, *Whole-Bible Connections*, and *Theological Soundings*. Then take time to reflect on the *Personal Implications* these sections may have for your walk with the Lord.

▶ Gospel Glimpses

THE GOSPEL MAKES US "NATURAL." In Romans 1:26–27, Paul comments on the sinfulness of homosexuality. He calls heterosexual relations "natural" and calls deviation from this "contrary to nature" and "shameless." Here Paul is highlighting how the inward bent of sin creates such dysfunction and disorder that we defy the sovereign lordship of Christ, pursuing abnormal and unnatural relations as if they were natural and normal. Elsewhere Paul writes that before salvation we "lived in the passions of our flesh, carrying out the desires of the body and the mind" (Eph. 2:3). In this same pattern, Jude writes that apart from Christ sinners will be "destroyed by all that they, like unreasoning animals, understand instinctively" (Jude 10). The corollary to this truth is that after salvation, even as we become more and more conformed to the image of Christ, we are also becoming more and more our true selves. As the fruit of the Spirit increases in us, God restores order within us. Our minds are renewed (Rom. 12:2). We learn to do the natural thing spiritually and the spiritual thing naturally.

GOD'S KINDNESS LEADS YOU TO REPENTANCE.[1] In yet another wonderful affirmation of where the source of power to change is found, Paul reminds us in Romans 2:4 that "God's kindness is meant to lead you to repentance." Not his law, not his berating, not his exasperation or his cajoling. His kindness! It is grace, that trains us to renounce ungodliness (Titus 2:11–12).

SPIRIT-WROUGHT INCLUSION. In Romans 2:29 Paul writes, "But a Jew is one inwardly, and circumcision is a matter of the heart, by the Spirit, not by the letter. His praise is not from man but from God." No act of obedience or merit, no matter how religious, earns us favor with God. Nothing we can do will earn us inclusion in God's good graces. God's good graces grant us inclusion! And so the identifying marker is not outward manifestations, which as in the case of the Pharisees may belie the deadness inside, but rather the spiritual work that takes place in the heart. God's people are those in whom his Spirit resides, applying the atoning[2] work of Christ and sanctifying[3] believers over time. By virtue of this action, God is saving both Jews and non-Jews, however irreligious they may at first be.

Whole-Bible Connections

IDOLATRY. Paul shows us that the fundamental problem of human existence is the worship of false gods. Idolatry is the root of sin. He outlines it this way: "Claiming to be wise, they became fools, and exchanged the glory of the immortal God for images resembling mortal man and birds and animals and creeping things. . . . They exchanged the truth about God for a lie and worshiped and served the creature rather than the Creator, who is blessed forever!" (Rom. 1:22–23, 25). Human beings are never *not* worshiping. John Calvin has said that our hearts are "idol factories," and the story of Israel in the Old Testament certainly bears this out, as God's people continually struggle to trust the Lord but again and again lapse into idolatry.

DIVINE SOVEREIGNTY. There are many provocative claims in Paul's letter to the Romans, right from the start. Consider these verses from Romans 1: "Therefore God gave them up in the lusts of their hearts to impurity" (v. 24); "For this reason God gave them up to dishonorable passions" (v. 26); and "God gave them up to a debased mind to do what ought not to be done" (v. 28). God is "giving up" unrepentant sinners to their sin. In allowing sin to persist and harden in a person's heart, God maintains his sovereignty[4] in a way that does not negate human responsibility. One of the clearest places we see this is in God's dealing with Pharaoh in the book of Exodus. Several times we read that Pharaoh hardened his heart (Ex. 8:15, 32), but we also read that *God* hardened Pharaoh's heart (Ex. 4:21, 7:3, 9:12). So which was it? In the mystery of God's sovereignty and human responsibility, we learn that in effect the answer is "both." Sinners are responsible for their hard hearts, yet God is sovereign over human activity.

Theological Soundings

GENERAL REVELATION. Romans 1:19–20 sounds very similar to Psalm 19:1. The theological concept at work there is commonly called the doctrine of "general revelation." This idea, drawn from the Scriptures, is that God effectively reveals himself in the created world. The doctrine of general revelation does not claim that everything we need to know about God and his gospel in Christ is intelligible from the natural world—gospel knowledge necessitates what is called "special revelation," which refers to God's Word in the flesh (Jesus) and God's Word written down (the Bible). General revelation does mean, however, that there is enough of God's glory revealed in creation to leave sinners "without excuse" for their idolatry and unbelief (1:20).

"OBEY THE TRUTH." Romans 2:6–8 posits another counterintuitive truth. The truth of the gospel is not law or instructions or advice. It is news. It is not essentially something to obey but something to believe. Yet here Paul uses the curious phrase "obey the truth." The phrase "obey the gospel" appears elsewhere in the Scriptures (Rom. 10:16; 2 Thess. 1:8; 1 Pet. 4:17). What is meant here? Perhaps this: the first thing to *do* is to keep foremost in our minds that the saving work is already *done*. Let us obey—let us *heed*—that truth. Let us believe and live in a way that demonstrates that we believe the gospel is true.

NATURAL LAW. In Romans 2:12–16, Paul indicts all people under the reality of indwelling[5] sin. The special revelation of God's commandments explicitly reveals what is right and what is wrong. We hear clearly in the law what honors God and commends his holiness. And yet even those without the law have some awareness of right and wrong. We call this reality "natural law" because it tells us that even unbelievers are fundamentally and innately aware of justice, fairness, transgression, and morality.

Personal Implications

Take time to reflect on the implications of Romans 1:18–3:20 for your own life today. Make notes below on the personal implications for your walk with the Lord of (1) the *Gospel Glimpses*, (2) the *Whole-Bible Connections*, (3) the *Theological Soundings*, and (4) this passage as a whole.

1. Gospel Glimpses

2. Whole-Bible Connections

3. Theological Soundings

_____

_____

_____

_____

_____

_____

_____

_____

4. Romans 1:18–3:20

_____

_____

_____

_____

_____

_____

_____

▶ **As You Finish This Unit . . .**

Take a moment to ask for the Lord's blessing and help as you continue in this study of Romans. And take a moment also to look back through this unit of study, to reflect on some key things that the Lord may be teaching you.

Definitions

[1] **Repentance** – A complete change of heart and mind regarding one's overall attitude toward God and one's individual actions. True regeneration and conversion is always accompanied by repentance.

[2] **Atonement** – The reconciliation of a person with God, often associated with the offering of a sacrifice. Through his death and resurrection, Jesus Christ made atonement for the sins of believers. His death satisfied God's just wrath against sinful humanity, just as OT sacrifices symbolized substitutionary death as payment for sin.

[3] **Sanctification** – The process of being conformed to the image of Jesus Christ through the work of the Holy Spirit. This process begins immediately after regeneration and continues throughout a Christian's life, finally resulting in glorification.

[4] **Sovereignty** – Supreme and independent power and authority. Sovereignty over all things is a distinctive attribute of God (1 Tim. 6:15–16). He directs all things to carry out his purposes (Rom. 8:28–29).

[5] **Indwelling** – In Scripture, the word refers to the presence of Christ and the Holy Spirit within believers (Rom. 8:9–11; Eph. 3:16–19). This presence enables Christians to love (1 John 4:8–12) and to overcome sin, which also indwells believers but no longer defines them (Rom. 8:4–11).

WEEK 4: THE SAVING RIGHTEOUSNESS OF GOD

Romans 3:21–4:25

The Place of the Passage

Every good gospel presentation must tell us the bad news before it tells us the good news. This is what makes the good news so good. There is something terribly wrong with us and with the world. Thus far in Paul's letter to the church in Rome, he has been explaining just what that problem is—the rebellious transgression[1] of God's righteousness revealed generally in creation, universally in our consciences (dead though they are), and especially and specifically in the Scriptures. Paul has revealed and reaffirmed that we are sinners, following our perverted instincts into more and more death. The only justifiable response to our sin against God's righteousness is his right and just wrath. But that is the bad news; the gospel means "good news." In Romans 3:21–4:25, Paul articulates the heart of this great news of the gospel: God's remarkable and gracious response to our sin, and also how this response does not diminish or contravene but rather upholds his righteousness.

The Big Picture

Paul explains how sinners can be saved from God's wrath and counted as righteous before him through faith in Christ's atoning work.

Reflection and Discussion

Read through the complete passage for this study, Romans 3:21–4:25. Then review the shorter passages below and write your own notes on the following questions. (For further background, see the *ESV Study Bible*, pages 2163–2165; also available online at esv.org.)

1. God's Righteousness in the Death of Jesus (3:21–26)

The law of God is a great equalizer. The ground is level at the foot of the cross, because, since all have sinned and fallen short of God's glory (3:23), all need Jesus. How is God's righteousness manifested in Jesus Christ (3:21–22)?

How can God be called just if he passes over sins (3:25–26)?

2. Righteousness by Faith for Jews and Gentiles (3:27–31)

What is it about the nature of faith that precludes boasting (3:27)?

Paul is clear that salvation comes to us as a gift received by faith, not by works, but at the same time that God's commandments are not abolished. How does justification by faith uphold the law?

3. Abraham as the Father of Jews and Gentiles (4:1–25)

In 4:9–11, what does Paul point out about the order of Abraham's faith and his circumcision2? Why is this significant for our lives today?

Reflect on 4:19. What is the connection between Abraham's seeing his own aged body and Sarah's barrenness, and his realization that he could not find strength through the law?

Read through the following three sections on *Gospel Glimpses, Whole-Bible Connections*, and *Theological Soundings*. Then take time to reflect on the *Personal Implications* these sections have for your walk with the Lord.

Gospel Glimpses

GRACE. The "spiritual operating system" of the Christian's salvation and indeed his or her entire Christian life is grace.[3] Grace is sometimes defined as God's undeserved favor, and that is true. Grace can also be defined in terms of Jesus Christ himself. In Romans 3:24–25, Paul proclaims something astounding. We wretched sinners stand before God's unfathomable holiness with utter need, with nothing to offer except poverty of spirit, a depravity of such totality that God would be completely justified in pouring out an eternity of wrath upon us. But instead he pours out that wrath upon his Son, Jesus Christ, and thereby we are "justified by his grace as a gift." In God's grace, he justifies sinners and at the same time validates his own righteousness because he *has* punished us—in Christ!

GRACE AND LAW. In Romans 4:9–10 Paul once again confirms the necessary order of God's grace and our obedience to God's commands. He points out that Abraham was circumcised *after* his faith was credited to him as righteousness. We must see that the obedience of circumcision was a sign of an already existing faith—this act of obedience was the fruit of Abraham's salvation, not the cause of it. In the same way, we must make sure, as Martin Luther puts it, not to "muddle grace and law." We are not set free *by* our obedience; we are set free *to* and *for* obedience.

IMPUTATION. Paul uses the phrase "counted to him as righteousness" in Romans 4:22–25 and goes on to say that our faith is "counted" to us as righteousness. This phrase expresses the vital truth of what is called the imputation[4] of Christ's righteousness. We have no righteousness of our own. But when we believe in Christ's saving sufficiency, by faith we receive his saving righteousness as if it were our own! It is "counted to us," or credited to our account. As Christ takes our sin upon himself on the cross, receiving the wrath of the Father which is sin's due penalty, Christ's perfect obedience and sinless sacrifice and triumphant victory are reckoned to be ours (2 Cor. 5:21).

Whole-Bible Connections

JESUS AS FULFILLMENT. As Jesus is preaching the Sermon on the Mount, he announces that he has not come to abolish the law but to fulfill it (Matt. 5:17).

Paul provides an echo of this announcement in Romans 3:21–22 as he reveals that Christ is the manifestation of the righteousness of God that the law and prophets bore witness to. Because Jesus obeys the law perfectly, he fulfills its demands perfectly and becomes its perfect embodiment (Col. 2:17; Heb. 10:1). At Christ's transfiguration, Moses and Elijah appear beside him, emblematic of the law and prophets; yet by the end of that blazing vision, Jesus stands there alone. He is the fulfillment of all the biblical hope (Luke 24:27).

PSALM 32:1–2. In Romans 4:6–8, Paul quotes lines from one of David's psalms (Ps. 32:1–2). Paul shows that David's righteousness, like Abraham's, was credited to him by faith. The scandal of full forgiveness for sinners who trust in God was present even under the old covenant (see also Isa. 40:2; Mic. 7:19; Hab. 2:4). The Old Testament is flavored with eruptions of worship like Psalm 32:1–2, rejoicing in God's kindness to those who will trust in him despite their many failures.

THE PROMISES OF GOD. Abraham's faith in God's promise is commended in Romans 4:20–21. The promises of God, which are irrevocable (Rom. 11:29), sustained God's people throughout the history of redemption that unfolds in the Bible, and right up to the present day. Through sin, struggle, sacrifice, and suffering, even as God's people persistently dabble in faithlessness, God remains faithful. We can place our hope in him. And 2 Corinthians 1:20 tells us that the promises of God made to all the patriarchs and prophets find their "yes" in Jesus. If you are in Christ, every promise made to God's people down through the ages belongs to you as much as it did to its first hearers.

> ## Theological Soundings

PROPITIATION. Paul writes in Romans 3:25 that God put Christ forward "as a propitiation by his blood." Propitiation[5] is a great theological term that refers to the turning away of God's wrath. A propitiating sacrifice is one that makes its recipient "favorable" by averting God's wrath. So the offering of Christ on the "altar" of the cross was a payment that made the wrathful God propitious, or favorably disposed, toward those who believe.

THE JUST GOD. Romans 3:26 makes a curious statement: "It was to show [God's] righteousness at the present time, so that he might be just and the justifier of the one who has faith in Jesus." In this verse we learn that in offering Christ up on the cross to be crushed for our sins (Isa. 53:5–6), God simultaneously accomplishes the forgiving of our sin and the maintaining of his own holiness. For justice was indeed meted out. It was meted out on the one who did not deserve it, but who stood in the place of those who did.

CREATION *EX NIHILO*. Romans 4:17 displays the omnipotence and eternality of God by affirming the biblical doctrine of creation, which is that our uncreated

God created all that is not himself from absolutely nothing. He spoke nonexistence into existence. The theological phrase often used to refer to this truth is the Latin phrase *ex nihilo*, which means "out of nothing," that is, when nothing was there before. In the context of Paul's letter to the Romans, we see not only the affirmation that God created the world *ex nihilo*, but that by his grace he even creates *ex nihilo* the faith we need in our hearts to receive Christ.

Personal Implications

Take time to reflect on the implications of Romans 3:21–4:25 for your own life today. Make notes below on the personal implications for your walk with the Lord of (1) the *Gospel Glimpses*, (2) the *Whole-Bible Connections*, (3) the *Theological Soundings*, and (4) this passage as a whole.

1. Gospel Glimpses

2. Whole-Bible Connections

3. Theological Soundings

4. Romans 3:21–4:25

_____

_____

_____

_____

_____

_____

_____

> ### As You Finish This Unit . . .

Take a moment to ask for the Lord's blessing and help as you continue in this study of Romans. And take a moment also to look back through this unit of study, to reflect on some key things that the Lord may be teaching you.

Definitions

[1] **Transgression** – A violation of a command or law.

[2] **Circumcision** – The ritual practice of removing the foreskin of an individual, which was commanded for all male Israelites in OT times as a sign of participation in the covenant God established with Abraham (Gen. 17:9–14).

[3] **Grace** – Unmerited favor, especially the free gift of salvation that God gives to believers through faith in Jesus Christ.

[4] **Impute** – To attribute something to someone or credit it to his or her account. Often refers to God's crediting to every believer the righteousness of Jesus Christ.

[5] **Propitiation** – The appeasement of wrath by the offering of a gift or sacrifice. Jesus made propitiation for the sins of humanity by his suffering and death (Rom. 3:25; Heb. 2:17; 1 John 2:2; 4:10).

Week 5:
Hope as a Result of Righteousness by Faith

Romans 5:1–21

▲

The Bible reveals the secret to inconceivable and unconquerable joy. It is this, according to Romans 5:20: if we are in Christ, our sin cannot outpace God's grace. In Romans 5, Paul continues to develop his grand gospel narrative, the epic story of the redemption that is available for sinners in Christ Jesus. Previously he has shown us the sinfulness of all mankind, Jew and non-Jew alike. Then he showed us that God demonstrates his righteousness even in the forgiving of sins because he has placed the punishment for those sins on his sinless Son. This is how God's righteousness comes not to condemn us but to save us! As the plot thickens in Romans 5, Paul begins to explore the implications and applications of the gospel announcement that God saves sinners. From here, through Romans 6 and beyond, Paul will go on to discuss why the gospel of grace outlined in Romans 1–5 promotes holiness rather than a license to sin.

The Big Picture

Romans 5 preaches a comfort and peace surpassing each and every earthly circumstance, placing the Christian who is justified by faith in a place of utter security and hope.

Reflection and Discussion

Read through the complete passage for this study, Romans 5:1–21. Then review the shorter passages below and write your own notes on the following questions. (For further background, see the *ESV Study Bible*, pages 2165–2167; also available online at esv.org.)

1. Assurance of Hope (5:1–11)

Paul's hope is not a speculative thing. It is a joyful expectation. Why?

How is Christian hope (5:2) different from the way most people think of hope?

Why does Paul say that hope does not put us to shame (5:5)?

How is good character related to good hope (5:4)?

What is the significance of noting that Christ died for us "while we were still sinners" (5:8)?

2. Hope in Christ's Triumph over Adam's Sin (5:12–21)

According to 5:12–14, how would people know sin was in the world before the law revealed it? What does this tell us about sin?

Paul vividly contrasts the grace in Christ with the sin in Adam. How is the free gift of grace not like the trespass (5:15)? What does it mean to be under the realm of Christ rather than under the realm of Adam?

What does Paul mean when he says "the law came in to increase the trespass" (5:20)?

Read through the following three sections on *Gospel Glimpses*, *Whole-Bible Connections*, and *Theological Soundings*. Then take time to reflect on the *Personal Implications* these sections have for your walk with the Lord.

Gospel Glimpses

CONDEMNATION FOR EVERYONE, LIFE FOR ANYONE. In Romans 5:18, Paul explains how sin has come to "all" because of Adam's sin and how, similarly, the grace of God in Christ comes to all. The Bible clearly teaches that God's wrath remains on those who do not receive God's gift of grace by faith, and that they will therefore receive eternal condemnation for their sins. Therefore, this verse should not be seen as teaching universalism[1] (the belief that every individual person will be saved). Rather, in light of Paul's discussions throughout Romans of the roles of Jews and Gentiles (non-Jews) in God's saving purposes, this verse should be seen in terms of "transculturalism," that is, it teaches that people of all kinds will be saved. Paul's use of the expression "the many" in verse 19 helps to clarify this. The gospel is for "the many," Jews and Gentiles alike.

"ABOUNDING GRACE." The promise of Romans 5:20–21 is thrilling. Because those saved by grace through faith are freely and fully justified, having been forgiven, counted righteous, and reconciled to God the Father, no sin can overcome God's abundant grace. He is more ready to forgive than we are to sin. And oh, how prone to sin we are! We are chomping at the bit, aren't we? Wretches as we are, who will rescue us? Praise be to God for his glorious grace (Rom. 7:24–25). There is more grace in him than sin in us.

Whole-Bible Connections

THE LAST ADAM. Romans 5:14 offers us a glimpse of a truth that Paul more directly reveals in 1 Corinthians 15:22, where he writes, "as in Adam all die, so also in Christ shall all be made alive." As sin and death entered the world through Adam, grace and life entered the world through Jesus. In this way, Jesus is the second (or "last") Adam (1 Cor. 15:45). This template, what is sometimes called "typology,"[2] is seen throughout the Old Testament. All of the heroes of the faith were stained by Adam's sin. Jesus, the sinless redeemer of what Adam corrupted, is the truer and better Adam, the prophet, priest, and king that we all so desperately need.

Theological Soundings

CHRISTUS VICTOR. On the cross, Jesus Christ absorbs the wrath of God, the due punishment for our sins, and thereby satisfies the justice of God and purchases our pardon. This is often called "penal substitution," because it describes the fulfillment of the Old Testament's blood sacrifices as a punishment (penal) in the place of the sinner (substitution). But though penal substitution is the center of Christ's atoning work, the Scriptures explain it in other important ways as well. One of these views of the atonement is traditionally called *Christus Victor*, a Latin phrase that essentially means what it looks like— Christ the Victor. Jesus on the cross became not just the propitiating sacrifice for sin but the conqueror triumphing over sin and the powers of evil. His crucifixion was in reality a coronation! Colossians 2:15 and Hebrews 2:14–15 speak to Christ's triumph clearly, but there are also shades of it throughout Romans 5 in Paul's use of "reign." Sin reigned in us before Christ died. At the cross, Christ reigned over sin, triumphed over the evil rule, and thereby showed himself, even on the cross, Lord over us.

"TO INCREASE THE TRESPASS." We can always count on the Bible to "shoot straight" with us. No one is as honest with us *about us* as God is. So when Paul writes in Romans 5:20, "Now the law came in to increase the trespass," we have no choice but to admit what is true of us. When someone tells us not to do something, we instinctively want to do it. Ever heard the phrase "Rules are meant to be broken"? Here is a convicting truth about the law: it doesn't just reveal our sin; in many ways it provokes us to sin even more. Not because the law is bad, but because *we* are. What amazing grace that God would forgive our perverse tendency to turn even his holy law into an opportunity for sinning.

Personal Implications

Take time to reflect on the implications of Romans 5 for your own life today. Make notes below on the personal implications for your walk with the Lord of (1) the *Gospel Glimpses*, (2) the *Whole-Bible Connections*, (3) the *Theological Soundings*, and (4) this passage as a whole.

1. Gospel Glimpses

2. Whole-Bible Connections

3. Theological Soundings

4. Romans 5

As You Finish This Unit . . .

Take a moment to ask for the Lord's blessing and help as you continue in this study of Romans. And take a moment also to look back through this unit of study, to reflect on some key things that the Lord may be teaching you.

Definitions

[1] **Universalism** – The unbiblical belief that all people will be saved from eternal damnation, regardless of whether or not they come to faith in Christ.

[2] **Typology** – A method of biblical interpretation in which a real historical object, place, or person is recognized as a pattern or foreshadowing (a "type") of some later object, place, or person. For example, the Bible presents Adam as a "type" of Christ (Rom. 5:14).

WEEK 6: THE TRIUMPH OF GRACE

Romans 6:1–7:25

The Place of the Passage

Romans 6:1–7:25 is somewhat of a "hinge" for the letter to the Romans, as Paul continues to elaborate on the implications of the gospel of justification by faith in Jesus Christ. Paul will return to explore the promises of God in relation to the salvation of Israel and in relation to the mission to the Gentiles once again in subsequent chapters, but in Romans 6–7 Paul zooms in to show us how God's grace not only justifies but actually changes people. Romans 6:1–7:25 answers the question "What do we do, then, knowing the truth of Romans 1:1–5:21?" While Paul will later work out the practical details of Christian living, the *theology* of change in Romans 6–7 is equally crucial. Here Paul is showing that grace is powerful enough both to save us from sin and to save us *to* obedience.

The Big Picture

Romans 6:1–7:25 explores the power of union with Christ and the impotence of the law in sanctification.

Reflection and Discussion

Read through the complete passage for this study, Romans 6:1–7:25. Then review the shorter passages below and write your own notes on the following questions. (For further background, see the *ESV Study Bible*, pages 2167–2169; also available online at esv.org.)

1. The Triumph of Grace over the Power of Sin (6:1–23)

How does Paul refute the idea that, since more sinning results in more grace, we should sin all the more (5:20–6:11)?

Paul moves from the indicative (what is true) of 6:1–11 to the imperative (what to do) of 6:12–14. How would you summarize each of these two sections? What is the relationship between them? Is the imperative built on the indicative, or the indicative on the imperative?

If Paul is telling believers to pursue sacrificial obedience, why is he saying we are not under the law (6:14)?

How does Paul employ the metaphor of slavery throughout 6:15–23? Is it possible not to be a slave to something?

2. The Triumph of Grace over the Power of the Law (7:1–25)

Comparing our connection to the law to the marital covenant (7:1–6) is not exactly flattering to marriage, but Paul is revealing something powerful about a Christian's relationship to the law. What is the basic point of Paul's illustration in these verses?

What are some examples of the law arousing sinful passions (7:5)?

We can get the mistaken impression, because of all the negative implications of the law's functions, that the law is only bad. For what reason(s) does Paul say the law is good (7:12)?

Thinking personally, how have you seen the inner struggle Paul describes in 7:18–23 in your own life?

What are your primary means of encouragement and strength during such struggles?

Read through the following three sections on *Gospel Glimpses, Whole-Bible Connections*, and *Theological Soundings*. Then take time to reflect on the *Personal Implications* these sections have for your walk with the Lord.

Gospel Glimpses

THE RESURRECTION TO COME. In Romans 6:5–11, Paul asserts, based on the believer's union with Christ, that we have not only died to sin; we have also been raised with Christ. In one sense, we enjoy this resurrection life now because we have eternal life now. But there is also the future tense, the great day to come, in which we will be transformed and will put off these mortal bodies to put on immortal bodies (1 Corinthians 15). In the resurrection to come, purchased by Christ in *his* resurrection, we will inherit a restored earth and enjoy the grace of God, free from sin and death for all eternity.

"UNDER GRACE." When Paul writes in Romans 6:14 that we are "not under law but under grace," he does not mean that we have no obligation to obey God anymore. In fact, he has just spent thirteen verses saying the opposite of that. What he's referring to is the "engine" of obedience. The reality of the sin-forgiven life is that we now live under the dominion of grace. The result is that we live in increasing conformity to the righteousness of God and increasing awareness of and conviction about our failure to fully measure up to God's standard. Under the grace that pardons all our sin, sin does not abound, or else it is not grace that is in charge, but sin itself. This is what Paul is getting at when he talks about our union with Christ making us "slaves to righteousness" (6:15–23).

Whole-Bible Connections

FREEDOM FOR THE CAPTIVES. Paul's exulting in the freedom that grace provides to those who were in bondage to sin is a Christ-centered echo of what is promised in Isaiah 61: "the LORD has anointed me to bring good news to the poor; he has sent me to bind up the brokenhearted, to proclaim liberty to the captives, and the opening of the prison to those who are bound" (Isa. 61:1). Jesus applies this to himself in the synagogue in Luke 4:16-21. The true King has come to announce liberty.

THE LAW. The first command from God to his people comes in the Garden of Eden (Gen. 2:16–17). Our first parents broke that law, and we humans have been disobeying God ever since. Despite God's lavish goodness to his people, which always precedes his law-giving (e.g., Ex. 20:2), we are inveterate law-breakers. In Jesus, however, the law is finally kept (Matt. 5:17). United to him, believers are credited with Christ's account (that is, his righteousness is imputed to them and becomes theirs), and they are declared free, once and for all, from the prospect of an eternal penalty for sin (2 Cor. 5:21; Phil. 3:9).

Theological Soundings

ANTINOMIANISM. In the opening verses of Romans 6, Paul is rebuking a reaction to the doctrine of free grace that is often referred to as "antinomianism,"[1] which means "against the law." The logic goes like this: If I have total forgiveness for my sin, and if in fact the more sin abounds, the more grace abounds (5:20), then am I not free to sin all the more so that grace may continue to abound (6:1)? Paul finds this logic appalling. Though it claims to champion radical grace, such a sentiment is wicked and reveals a heart that has not truly been touched by redeeming grace. Grace is the antidote not only to legalism[2] but also to license, for Christians have been united to Christ (6:5). The professed believer who claims that grace gives him license to sin with abandon is not a believer at all.

UNION WITH CHRIST. Here is one of the major themes of the New Testament, and the overarching salvific result of Christ's atoning work for God's elect. In

Romans 6:3–11, Paul grounds his thinking in the reality that by God's grace received through faith, a sinner is in fact united to Christ. The recurring biblical phrases "in Christ" and "in him" speak to this eternal reality. We are "hidden with Christ in God" (Col. 3:3). We have died with Jesus and we have risen with him. Now he is in us (Col. 1:27; 1 John 3:9) and we are in him (Acts 17:28; 1 John 4:13). First John 3:24 says, "Whoever keeps his commandments abides in God, and God in him." How can Paul assert that we are free to stop sinning and to start obeying? Because we are united with God's own Son, obedience from our heart, though not unopposed, is now natural to us.

THE BELIEVER'S NEW NATURE. Romans 7 shows us who we *were* and who we now *are*. Is a Christian a saint or a sinner? Does he or she have a new nature or a sin nature? The answer is: yes—*in that order*. We must hold these two realities in tension. We are both saints and sinners. We are redeemed sinners. The reformer Martin Luther used the provocative phrase *simul iustus et peccator* to describe this strange state of affairs: we are "at the same time righteous and sinner." This is an important doctrine because it reflects the biblical reality Paul sets forth in Romans 7, and also because it gives us both humility and confidence. If I believe I am only a sinner but not a saint, I will remain prone to self-pity and despair, and joy will be elusive. If I believe I am only a saint but not a sinner, I am neck-deep in pride, cloaking myself in the rags of self-justification. And yet, while both of these realities are true, we must see that the Bible teaches that what now fundamentally defines me is the new life I have been given in Christ. While I remain fallen as long as I live, my fundamental identity is as a redeemed, new-hearted child of God.

Personal Implications

Take time to reflect on the implications of Romans 6:1–7:25 for your own life today. Make notes below on the personal implications for your walk with the Lord of (1) the *Gospel Glimpses*, (2) the *Whole-Bible Connections*, (3) the *Theological Soundings*, and (4) this passage as a whole.

1. Gospel Glimpses

2. Whole-Bible Connections

3. Theological Soundings

4. Romans 6:1–7:25

As You Finish This Unit . . .

Take a moment to ask for the Lord's blessing and help as you continue in this study of Romans. And take a moment also to look back through this unit of study, to reflect on some key things that the Lord may be teaching you.

Definitions

[1] **Antinomianism** – The false belief that OT moral laws are no longer necessary or binding for those living under grace (see Rom. 6:1–2).

[2] **Legalism** – Requirements that go beyond the commands of Scripture; or the unbiblical belief that works are the means of becoming right with God.

WEEK 7:
LIFE IN THE SPIRIT

Romans 8:1–39

▲

The eighth chapter of Romans is one of the most powerful passages of Scripture. Up to this point, Paul has not highlighted the work of the Holy Spirit in the believer's life, but in this great text, perhaps the highest peak among all the spiritual heights visited in the epistle, the role of the Spirit in applying the saving work of Christ in justification and beyond begins to take vibrant shape. There are two extraordinary bookends to the chapter. Paul reveals how our union with Christ not only justifies us but provides for us the indwelling presence of the Spirit of Christ. Paul gives a panoramic view of the riches of Christ in our adoption, our identity, our sanctification, our strength in times of suffering and weakness, and our final destiny. Romans 8 summarizes and drives home to the human heart the implications of our salvation presented in Romans 1–7 and prepares the way for Paul to discuss the relationship between

Jews and Gentiles in God's plan (Romans 9–11, 15) and the practical outworking of life in the Spirit (Romans 12–14).

The Big Picture

If we are united with Christ, adopted by God, and indwelt by the Spirit, then we are as secure as Christ himself is.

Reflection and Discussion

Read through the complete passage for this study, Romans 8. Then review the shorter passages below and write your own notes on the following questions. (For further background, see the *ESV Study Bible*, pages 2170–2172; also available online at esv.org.)

1. Life in the Spirit (8:1–17)

What has been said prior to Romans 8:1 that leads Paul to say that believers are under no condemnation? What role does union with Christ play in this verse?

If Jesus was sinless, why does Paul say he was "in the likeness of sinful flesh" (8:3)?

What are some practical ways to set your mind on the "things of the Spirit" (8:5–8)?

According to 8:13, is sanctification God's work or ours? Consider also 1 Corinthians 15:10; Philippians 2:12–13; and Colossians 1:29.

What does it mean to be an heir (8:16–17)? What are the benefits of being fellow heirs with Christ?

2. The Assurance of Hope (8:18–39)

What does 8:19–22 tell us about sin?

What are some ways we might *mis*interpret Romans 8:28?

How is Romans 8:28 similar to Philippians 4:13?

What might Paul have in mind in the "all things" of 8:32?

How can those being "killed all the day long" (8:36) be "more than conquerors" (8:37)?

Read through the following three sections on *Gospel Glimpses, Whole-Bible Connections*, and *Theological Soundings*. Then take time to reflect on the *Personal Implications* these sections have for your walk with the Lord.

Gospel Glimpses

"IN THE SPIRIT." Romans 8:9 explains the spiritual reality of the believer's union with Christ. If we are "in Christ," then we live not in the flesh but "in the Spirit." While we still sin, even as believers, we are no longer defined by the flesh—that is, by the natural, base, sinful demands of self. And if we are in the Spirit, it means that the Spirit is in *us*. The Spirit enables us to receive by faith the finished work of Christ, and then he "takes up residence" in us. Those who are born again have been consecrated by the Spirit, having become temples for his abiding presence (1 Cor. 6:19). This indwelling presence fuels our growth in godliness and in our producing the Spirit's fruit (Gal. 5:22–23).

ASSURANCE. Is it true that once we are born again, we will not revert to a state of spiritual death? Throughout Romans 8, Paul confirms the abiding confidence believers can have in Christ and the eternal life he imparts to his people. In Romans 8:1, he says there is no condemnation for believers. Romans 8:11 says we will receive immortal resurrection life. Romans 8:28 says everything is working toward the good for believers. Romans 8:31 reasons that God's favor is too large for any objections. And then, finally, climactically, and unequivocally, Paul says in Romans 8:35–39 that nothing can separate us from God's love, not even death and not even our own sin. God does not lie; he keeps his promises. So those who are justified will be glorified (Rom. 8:30)—not because we are faithful, but because God is. Paul puts the verb in the past tense to make the point that, being promised, it is as good as done.

DIVINE INTERCESSION. Now here is a great gospel truth! We learn in Romans 8:26–27 that the Spirit intercedes[1] for us. We learn in Romans 8:34 that Jesus himself intercedes for us. The Spirit intercedes by articulating to the Father the groanings from deep within our soul that we are not even able to put into words. The Son intercedes by showing the Father the merits of his death and resurrection. In effect, the Spirit and Son are both praying for us. What an astonishing and compelling reason for hope and confidence!

Whole-Bible Connections

HEIRS. Paul develops an interesting theme in his exploration of the spiritual blessings we receive in Christ (Rom. 8:16–17). Because we are joined to Christ, his Father becomes our Father. And since his Father is our Father, we receive the blessings of sonship, becoming co-heirs with our elder brother, Jesus. This is a crucial fulfillment of something we see throughout the Old Testament stories. Traditionally, the oldest son in a family receives the highest honor among siblings; he is the recipient of the birthright. But over and over again, the older brothers in the biblical narratives fail and fall. They are shown to be utterly incompetent and very often brutally cruel. So God, in a display of his grace, consistently uses "younger brothers," the ones you would not expect to carry out his redemptive plans. Think of Abel, Jacob, Joseph, and David—all younger brothers who are uniquely favored by God. When we get to the New Testament, Jesus tells a parable about a younger brother who selfishly leaves his family (Luke 15:11–32). Here is another opportunity for the older brother to redeem "older brotherhood," but the older brother in the story is cold and proud. Again we are left yearning for the good older brother. Enter Jesus. He is the perfect older brother who loves his sinful siblings, seeks their good, lays down his life for them, isn't ashamed to be united to them (Heb. 2:11), and in the end shares all the riches that are his birthright with his brothers and sisters. We are co-heirs with Jesus—of the entire earth (Matt. 5:5).

Theological Soundings

FOREKNOWLEDGE. There is a key word in Romans 8:29 that is too often and easily missed, and it is this: "whom." A major misunderstanding of God's foreknowledge by many is that it refers to God's foreknowing who will believe in Christ and then electing them based on that decision. But the verse does not say that God foreknows *what* will happen; it says that he foreknows *who* will "happen." It is of course true that God has foreknowledge of all future events. That is part of his omniscience.[2] But in his eternal fatherhood and omniscience, he foreknows relationally those who are his children, which is to say, he knows them inside and out. He knows who they are and what they will be like, and he has designated that, however sinful they are, they are nevertheless *his*. So the foreknowledge in Romans 8:29 is not factual foreknowledge so much as relational foreknowledge. In a word, it is love. We are lovingly chosen in Christ before the foundation of the world (Eph. 1:3–4).

THE *ORDO SALUTIS*. Sometimes called the golden chain of salvation, Romans 8:30 outlines a sort of chronology of the believer's salvation process. Theologians sometimes refer to this as the *ordo salutis*, a Latin phrase that means "order of salvation." When God predestines[3] someone to salvation, you can be sure he will call that person. And if he calls him, he will respond in the faith needed to be justified. And if he is justified, he will be glorified. Paul even puts the glorification of the believer in the past tense, as we saw, indicating that because it is promised and vicariously accomplished in Christ's resurrection and ascension, it is already secured. It is a foregone conclusion.

THE RESTORATION OF ALL THINGS. "Behold, I am making all things new," Jesus proclaims in Revelation 21:5. God's ultimate plan is not to scrap the earth and throw it into the waste bin like a crumpled piece of paper. He is renewing and will renew it. His plan is for the earth—this earth—to be covered with his glory "as the waters cover the sea" (Hab. 2:14). Every nook and cranny will be filled with his glory. When Adam sinned, the land was cursed too. That's how serious and consequential human sin is. But God will not let our sin conquer his plan for creation. Romans 8:19–23 shows this. The creation groans under its curse, but not in death throes; rather, in birth pangs. The whole cosmos is ripe with its future self. It is groaning for release. And one day, when Christ returns, we will receive with our King his dominion over a new heaven and a new earth. Just as Adam's sin and our inheritance of it infected the entire created order, so too does Christ's atoning work and our reception of it restore the entire created order.

Personal Implications

Take time to reflect on the implications of Romans 8 for your own life today. Make notes below on the personal implications for your walk with the Lord of (1) the *Gospel Glimpses*, (2) the *Whole-Bible Connections*, (3) the *Theological Soundings*, and (4) this passage as a whole.

1. Gospel Glimpses

2. Whole-Bible Connections

3. Theological Soundings

4. Romans 8:1–39

As You Finish This Unit . . .

Take a moment to ask for the Lord's blessing and help as you continue in this study of Romans. And take a moment also to look back through this unit of study, to reflect on some key things that the Lord may be teaching you.

Definitions

[1] **Intercede** – To appeal to one person on behalf of another. Often used with reference to prayer.

[2] **Omniscience** – An attribute of God that describes his complete knowledge and understanding of all things at all times.

[3] **Predestination** – God's sovereign choice of people for redemption and eternal life. Also referred to as "election."

Week 8: God's Promises to Israel

Romans 9:1–33

The Place of the Passage

Paul begins his letter to the Romans with a revelation of how the righteousness of God is revealed against the sins of Jews and Gentiles alike. One's ethnic status has no bearing on one's level of sinfulness (Romans 1–3). He then transitions to talk about the triumph of grace over sin that is needed by, and available to, both Jews and Gentiles (Romans 4–5). Paul then explains how this saving grace changes us, by the Spirit, in a way the law cannot (Romans 6–8). In Romans 9 he returns to the question of Jew and Gentile again. If God chose Israel to be his special people, how can those who are not part of Israel share in the promises God made to Israel? This is the question that will engage Paul in Romans 9–11.

The Big Picture

Paul draws on the Old Testament narrative to show that God sovereignly chooses, by his own good pleasure and ultimately for his own glory, those who will believe in him.

> **Reflection and Discussion**

Read through the complete passage for this study, Romans 9. Then review the shorter passages below and write your own notes on the following questions. (For further background, see the *ESV Study Bible*, pages 2172–2174; also available online at esv.org.)

1. God's Sovereign Choice (9:1–29)

Paul is about to share some hard truths. Note first his tone and disposition in Romans 9:1–3. How would you describe it? What impact ought this tone have on our reading of the hard things ahead, or how this passage is preached or taught?

Why does Paul anticipate the inquiry about God's word failing (Romans 9:6)? Why might someone, especially a Jew, ask this?

According to Romans 9:8, how is it that one becomes a child of God?

If God is love (1 John 4:8), what might it mean that God "hated" Esau (9:13)?

According to Romans 9:17, what is God's purpose in his sovereign acting? What are some other biblical examples of this?

What is the common thread that Paul sees between the stories of Abraham, Isaac, Jacob, and Pharaoh?

2. Israel's Unbelief (9:30–33)

Do Jews and Gentiles attain righteousness in different ways? Explain your answer.

What are the "points of stumbling" over the issue of righteousness for us today? In other words, what objections or aversions do we all naturally have that make salvation by faith hard to understand?

Read through the following three sections on *Gospel Glimpses*, *Whole-Bible Connections*, and *Theological Soundings*. Then take time to reflect on the *Personal Implications* these sections have for your walk with the Lord.

Gospel Glimpses

SOVEREIGN MERCY. Romans 9:16 is unassailable encouragement: "So then it depends not on human will or exertion, but on God, who has mercy." When God sets his merciful designs on a person, he *will* capture them in his grace. This is a blow to human pride, yet it is also profound encouragement for those who feel weak and defeated by life, or even by their own sin. Look to Christ. Trust God. He is mighty to save. There is no separating us from his love (Rom. 8:38–39).

UPSIDE-DOWN APPROVAL. The gospel disrupts all our intuitive expectations about how God's favor is secured. Paul tells us in the last four verses of Romans 9 that so many Jews have stumbled because they sought to be right with God based on their own performance—"as if it were based on works" (9:32). Not only many Jews then but many of us today live in accord with our natural instincts, which insist on securing God's approval through some degree of self-generated moral contribution. The gospel confounds this natural reflex with the startling declaration that we are put right with God not by anything we bring to the table, but only and ever through "a righteousness that is by faith" (9:30).

Whole-Bible Connections

SUBSTITUTION. In Romans 9:3 Paul feels such love for his Jewish brothers and brokenness over their unbelief that he wishes he could be "accursed and cut off" for their sake if it would cause their salvation. This substitutionary wish is an echo of Moses' all the way back in Exodus 32:30–32 after the golden calf fiasco. Moses is so grieved by his people's sin and their feared destruction that he offers to be blotted out in their place if God would spare them. It is an impossible offer, but his cry is answered in Christ, who did substitute[1] himself for God's sinful people, becoming the curse for us (Gal. 3:13). Jesus is the true and final substitute.

A PEOPLE. What is God doing in history? Making a name for himself by gathering a people to himself. Paul makes this reality a major theme of his letter to the Romans, wanting his recipients to know that God has neither abandoned his promises to the Jews nor neglected the needs of the godless Gentiles; instead, he is assembling for himself a people out of every tongue, tribe, and nation (Rev. 5:9–10). And to make his case to the Jewish readers, he reminds them that this has been God's plan all along, throughout all the Scriptures (Rom. 9:24–29).

> ## Theological Soundings

ISRAEL AND THE CHURCH. The teaching of Romans 9:6–8 (and the verses following) is complex. Throughout Romans, Paul wants to make it clear that God's promises to Israel are irrevocable and certain. At the same time, he is opening up the understanding of those promises, explaining how they have been filled out in Christ and his gospel mission. This is not the same thing as saying that Christ's work is innovative, only that it was not entirely expected. Throughout the Gospels we see the followers of Jesus surprised by many of the things he did, leading up to and including his crucifixion. Yet at the same time we can see these things predicted in the Old Testament. So the clues were there all along, but the expectations did not match. We do not always see the things in the room clearly until the light is turned on. This is what the New Testament is—a light turned on by which to see everything, including the landscape of the Old Testament. Christ is himself the key that makes sense of all that God has been doing down through history. So when Paul gets to Romans 9:6–8, he wants us to know that God has not failed in his promises to Israel; it's just that "Israel" isn't limited to ethnic Israel. "Not all who are descended from Israel belong to Israel" (9:6). The children of the promise are descendants of Abraham. This is good tidings of great joy for all people—God keeps his promises to his people (Israel), and this includes non-Jews.

GOD'S SOVEREIGNTY IN SALVATION. Romans 9:11–18 develops a difficult yet profoundly comforting teaching: salvation is authored by God's sovereign grace, not by human free choice. Indeed, left to human free will, no one would ever choose God, for we are all desperately wicked and spiritually "dead" (Eph.

2:5). Paul teaches that those who trust in Jesus were predestined to do so in the wisdom of God's electing purposes, having been wooed in the course of their lives with invincible love. Anticipating our natural response of ascribing injustice to God's utter sovereignty, he then reminds us in a gentle rebuke that God is God. Because he is perfectly holy, whatever he does is the right thing to do, even if we do not understand or approve of it. We must let him be God. If we dictate to God what he must be like, then we are not in fact worshiping God—we are worshiping an idol, for it is a god of our own making. Moreover, the ultimate purpose in God's sovereignty over salvation is the magnification of his own glory (Rom. 9:17). When we insist on salvation by our own initiative, we proclaim our own glory, making God's saving purposes all about us, as if we were in charge of him at this point. Nevertheless, God's glory and our good are wonderfully bound together: "he exalts himself to show mercy to you" (Isa. 30:18).

Personal Implications

Take time to reflect on the implications of Romans 9 for your own life today. Make notes below on the personal implications for your walk with the Lord of (1) the *Gospel Glimpses*, (2) the *Whole-Bible Connections*, (3) the *Theological Soundings*, and (4) this passage as a whole.

1. Gospel Glimpses

---

2. Whole-Bible Connections

---

3. Theological Soundings

_____
_____
_____
_____
_____
_____
_____
_____

4. Romans 9:1–33

_____
_____
_____
_____
_____
_____
_____
_____

As You Finish This Unit . . .

Take a moment to ask for the Lord's blessing and help as you continue in this study of Romans. And take a moment also to look back through this unit of study, to reflect on some key things that the Lord may be teaching you.

Definitions

[1] **Substitutionary atonement** – The core reason for Jesus' death on the cross: identifying with his Father's will, Jesus offered himself to die as a substitute for believers. He took upon himself the punishment they deserve and thereby reconciled them to God.

Week 9: God's Righteousness in His Plans for Jews and Gentiles

Romans 10:1–11:36

The Place of the Passage

The message of the gospel is for all peoples: for the Jews who sought but did not believe and for the Gentiles who did not seek at all. Paul knows this is controversial, especially for Jews, and he seems to discern rising tensions in the Roman church between Jewish and Greek believers. As a result, he makes his painstaking case in Romans 10:1–11:36 for the universal proclamation of the gospel of Jesus and the Jewish people's rejection of it. But God is faithful! His promises will not fail. In Romans 11, Paul discusses the importance of the remnant[1] of believers in Israel and how the incorporation of the Gentiles into their Christian community actually effects the salvation of "all Israel" (11:26).

The Big Picture

Romans 10:1–11:36 explains how the gospel is good news for people of all ethnicities and cultures, not just Jews, and then explores the implications of this point for the Jewish rejection of Jesus.

Reflection and Discussion

Read through the complete passage for this study, Romans 10:1–11:36. Then review the shorter passages below and write your own notes on the following questions. (For further background, see the *ESV Study Bible*, pages 2174–2178; also available online at esv.org.)

1. The Gospel Heard and Unheard (10:1–11:10)

Paul's broken heart and love for his Jewish brothers and sisters is once again evident in Romans 10:1. But because he loves them, he must be honest with and about them. They have much passion, but this zeal is not according to knowledge. How does Paul explain in 10:3 what kind of "knowledge" he is referring to in 10:2?

If you recall it, describe your moment of conversion. What circumstances led to your salvation, and how was the gospel preached?

What does Paul mean by the phrase "obeyed the gospel" (10:16)?

God is not passive. Though he does delight to respond to the pleas of his people, he does not sit back and wait to be summoned. He is active, ruling, and engaged in this world. Reflect on Romans 10:20. What are some other biblical examples you can think of that show God revealing himself to people who were not seeking him at all? What examples of God's own initiative do you see in your own life?

2. God's Righteousness in His Plan for Jews and Gentiles (11:11–32)

How does salvation come to Gentiles through the trespass of the Jews (11:11)?

What extended metaphor does Paul use throughout 11:17–24, and how does he use it?

Why is justification by faith antithetical to pride (11:20)?

Read Romans 11:26 again. What is "the way" Paul is saying all Israel will be saved?

3. Concluding Doxology (11:33–36)

How would you describe Paul's tone in these four verses? Why do you think he concludes in this way?

How would you define "glory" (11:36)?

Read through the following three sections on *Gospel Glimpses*, *Whole-Bible Connections*, and *Theological Soundings*. Then take time to reflect on the *Personal Implications* these sections have for your walk with the Lord.

Gospel Glimpses

THE SIMPLICITY OF THE GOSPEL. It is not easy to be saved. In fact, on our own steam, it's impossible (Rom. 8:7). So Christ accomplishes the work for us. How do we receive this work? Again, the exercise of faith is impossible without the enabling power at the new birth (John 3:3; Rom. 12:3; Eph. 2:8). But we have no hoops to jump through, no levels to climb, no performance to achieve. In fact, while trusting Christ is not easy, it is quite simple. In Romans 10:9, Paul writes, "If you confess with your mouth that Jesus is Lord and believe in your heart that God raised him from the dead, you will be saved." This is so simple, in fact, that Jesus implies that the kingdom is precisely for those of a childlike faith (Matt. 19:14)—trusting, vulnerable, unselfconscious. Even a mustard seed–sized amount of faith receives the mountain-moving power of the kingdom of God (Matt. 17:20). Every other religion and philosophy specifies steps and tips—*law*, in other words—to reach whatever they see as "salvation." Only Christianity says that the work is accomplished, and it is ours to simply believe. What good news!

PURE GRACE. "But if it is by grace, it is no longer on the basis of works; otherwise grace would no longer be grace," Paul writes in Romans 11:6. What is the ratio of grace to works needed to receive the justifying righteousness of Jesus Christ? One to zero. It is 100 percent grace that is needed. Otherwise grace would not be grace. The grace of God is not a down payment to get us started on an installment-plan salvation. It is not the push of a swing whose momentum must be maintained by our rocking. It is grace from beginning to end. Any compromise at this point undermines the whole of our salvation. For if we try to reinforce our eternal security by injecting just a little bit of personal morality into the mix, we reject and dishonor the perfect righteousness and finished work of Jesus Christ. This is good news because it gives us the freedom to be what we are without trying: sinful people desperately in need of grace for justification, sanctification, and glorification. And it's also good news because it means we will have the 100 percent pure, unadulterated grace we need to empower our repentance and godly living.

Whole-Bible Connections

GLOBAL REDEMPTION. "For there is no distinction between Jew and Greek; for the same Lord is Lord of all, bestowing his riches on all who call on him. For 'everyone who calls on the name of the Lord will be saved'" (Rom. 10:12–13). In Romans 3 Paul had used exactly the same phrase, "there is no distinction," to underscore the universality of sin: "there is no distinction: for all have sinned" (3:22–23). While in Romans 3 Paul said there is no distinction in who sins, in Romans 10 Paul says there is no distinction in who can be saved. The gospel is not for insiders. And this has been God's plan all along. God called Abraham to be a blessing to the nations (Gen. 12:1–3). This is reiterated by the prophets (e.g., Isa. 42:6; 49:6). Indeed, Paul quotes Joel 2:32 when he says that "everyone who calls on the name of the Lord will be saved" (Rom. 10:13). The result is that at the end of the Bible, when readers are given a glimpse into the new heavens and the new earth, we see "a great multitude that no one could number, from every nation, from all tribes and peoples and languages, standing before the throne and before the Lamb" (Rev. 7:9).

SPIRITUAL BLINDNESS. In Romans 11:8 Paul once again speaks to the blindness and deafness that those apart from God suffer from until the prison of their spiritual senses has been broken open. In this instance, he quotes Isaiah 29:10 and Deuteronomy 29:4 to demonstrate the old covenant examples of this spiritual defect. Indeed, in Isaiah 6:9–13, God calls the prophet Isaiah to a mission of preaching a message that not only falls on deaf ears and hostile hearts but actually creates them. And Jesus applies this same dynamic to his motivation in teaching in parables (Matt. 13:14–15). Paul is reminding his Jewish readers that even their hard-heartedness was not unforeseen by God. It is no surprise. And he wants all to know that faith comes by hearing, and that even effectual hearing is a gift of God's grace in the gospel (Rom. 10:17).

Theological Soundings

HUMAN RESPONSIBILITY IN EVANGELISM. For all that Paul has said about God's sovereignty in history and in salvation, the apostle does not allow this emphasis to undermine the compatible reality of human responsibility. While in Romans 9 Paul teaches us about God's sovereignty, in Romans 10 he teaches us that divine sovereignty coexists with our responsibility. Paul's reasoning in Romans 10:14–17 shows that God's sovereign will fuels, not replaces, the urgency of telling others the gospel of Jesus Christ. "How are they to believe in him of whom they have never heard?" (10:14). Indeed, the urgency of evangelism would be hindered if God were *not* sovereign, for then we would have no reason to hope that anyone would be brought from death to life by our preaching and witnessing.

ISRAEL AND LAST THINGS. Entire volumes have been written on the place of Israel and the wider world in God's plan for what is often called eschatology[2] or "the end times."[3] Many scholars believe that the unrepentance and disbelief of Jews yesterday and today is only a temporary predicament, that there will be a widespread revival within the Jewish people shortly before Christ's final return. This is certainly plausible, since Paul explains that the hardening that has come upon Israel, preventing them from seeing Jesus Christ as the Messiah, is only "partial" (11:25), and it is only "until the fullness of the Gentiles has come in." In Romans 11:29, he reiterates that God's calling on the Jewish people is irrevocable, just as earlier he has reminded us that God has not rejected his chosen people (11:1). On the other hand, it is also clear from the New Testament that many (if not all) of the promises made to ethnic Israel are now fulfilled in Christ and the church. Intelligent, Bible-believing Christians hold differing views on what all this means for the place of national, ethnic Israel within the eschatological landscape. Despite these differing views, Bible-believing Christians of all viewpoints agree that God keeps his promises. His plan to glorify every person who expresses faith in Christ, be they Jew or Greek, insider or outsider, is secure. This is grounds for great hope and joy as we anticipate the glorious future awaiting us in the new heavens and the new earth.

Personal Implications

Take time to reflect on the implications of Romans 10:1–11:36 for your own life today. Make notes below on the personal implications for your walk with the Lord of (1) the *Gospel Glimpses*, (2) the *Whole-Bible Connections*, (3) the *Theological Soundings*, and (4) this passage as a whole.

1. Gospel Glimpses

2. Whole-Bible Connections

3. Theological Soundings

4. Romans 10:1–11:36

As You Finish This Unit . . .

Take a moment to ask for the Lord's blessing and help as you continue in this study of Romans. And take a moment also to look back through this unit of study, to reflect on some key things that the Lord may be teaching you.

Definitions

[1] **Remnant** – In the Bible, a portion of people who remain after most others are destroyed by some catastrophe. The notion of a "remnant" can be found in various events recorded in Scripture, including the flood (Genesis 6–8) and the return of exiled Judah (Ezra 9).

[2] **Eschatology** – Study of the end times as described in the Bible. Includes such topics as the return of Christ, the period of tribulation, the resurrection and judgment of all people, and the millennial reign of Christ on earth.

[3] **The end times** – A time associated with events prophesied in Scripture to occur at the end of the world and the second coming of Christ—also known as "the last days." The New Testament teaches that in Christ, the last days have dawned. The "end times" can refer, then, to the entire period in between Christ's first and second comings.

WEEK 10:
LIVING IN LIGHT
OF THE GOSPEL

Romans 12:1–13:14

Where have we been so far in Paul's letter to the Roman church? First, he revealed the righteousness of God against the sin of all mankind. Then he revealed the implications of this truth for Jews and Gentiles. Next, he revealed the righteousness of God found in the gospel of the grace of Christ, along with the implications of that truth for Jews and Gentiles. All people, both Jew and Gentile, are unified in our common need for salvation. And so the antidote for this problem is the same for us all: Jesus Christ. Paul also has explained how God has been faithful to his promises to Israel. Now in chapter 12 Paul begins his practical instructions for holy living. Romans 12:1–13:14 is the "then" to the preceding chapters' "if." *If* this glorious gospel is true, *then* here is how believers should live in glad response. This structure is a pattern in Paul's other letters, too.

> ## The Big Picture

Romans 12:1–13:14 reveals what life in the Spirit looks like for the justified in their relationships with others, both in the church and in the government.

> ## Reflection and Discussion

Read through the complete passage for this study, Romans 12:1–13:14. Then review the shorter passages below and write your own notes on the following questions. (For further background, see the *ESV Study Bible*, pages 2178–2180; also available online at esv.org.)

1. The umbrella exhortation (12:1–2)

The overarching exhortation for 12:1–13:14 is given in the first two verses. These verses are the umbrella under which all that follows is included. What does Paul mean by a "living sacrifice"[1] (12:1)?

In what ways do you struggle most with conformity to the world (12:2)? What is Paul's antidote to being conformed to the world (12:2)? What might this look like in your present daily living?

2. Marks of the Christian Community (12:3–21)

In 12:3–8 we find one of four New Testament treatments of spiritual gifts. Skim the others: 1 Corinthians 12:7–10; 1 Corinthians 12:28; and Ephesians 4:11. What similarities and what differences do you observe? What do you perceive to be your own spiritual gifts? What would others say about you?

How can Paul *command* what appear to be *feelings*, such as love, fervency, or rejoicing (12:9–12)?

Why would Paul exhort us to rejoice with those who rejoice and weep with those who weep (12:15)? How do we see each of these in the life of Jesus?

Reflect on Romans 12:19. What is difficult about this verse? What is liberating?

3. Relating to Government (13:1–7)

How is Paul's instruction in 13:1–7 ultimately an act of faith?

What is Paul's theological reason for submitting to civil authority?

How does 13:1–7 fit with other places in the New Testament where faithfulness requires *not* submitting to authority (e.g., Acts 4:19–20; 5:29; 1 Pet. 2:20)?

4. The Law and Love (13:8–14)

How does love sum up the entire law?

What is Paul's broader point in utilizing the day/night imagery in 13:11–14?

_____

_____

_____

_____

_____

_____

What does Paul mean by "put on the Lord Jesus Christ" (13:14)? What are other texts in the New Testament that might be getting at the same idea?

_____

_____

_____

_____

_____

_____

Read through the following three sections on *Gospel Glimpses*, *Whole-Bible Connections*, and *Theological Soundings*. Then take time to reflect on the *Personal Implications* these sections have for your walk with the Lord.

Gospel Glimpses

ONE BODY. What a beautiful picture of reconciliation[2] and unity we receive in Romans 12! If individuals have been transformed and are growing in the image of Christ, then they are growing more and more into the picture of reconciliation that the church is called to embody. Only if we have been totally justified do we cease seeking to self-justify, which means we do not take vengeance, or operate in self-defense mode, or create opportunities for self-exaltation. Instead, walking in the confidence and humility of the gospel, we can love our neighbors well and submit ourselves to the whole of the body of Christ, providing a visible picture of the reconciling work of Christ's cross. This witness commends the gospel to those outside the church.

LOVE. Out of God's love he saves us. Out of our salvation, we love others. This is something the gospel creates as it answers the law's demands in every way. We see in the Ten Commandments a twofold division: vertical relationship with God (first four commandments) and horizontal relationship with our neighbor (last six commandments). Jesus sums it up by saying that the Great Commandment is "You shall love the Lord your God with all your heart and with all your soul and with all your strength and with all your mind, and your neighbor as yourself" (Luke 10:27). The gospel satisfies this, creating in our hearts, through God's love for us, love for God and love for our neighbor. "We love because he first loved us" (1 John 4:19).

Whole-Bible Connections

NONCONFORMITY. "Do not be conformed to this world . . . " (Rom. 12:2). What Paul champions as he opens Romans 12 is the spirit of alien residency that dates back to God's calling Abraham out of the nations to establish his covenant with one nation among the nations (Genesis 17) and carries over into Jesus' teaching to his disciples on being a city on a hill (Matt. 5:14). Jesus also prays along these lines in his prayer for his people at the end of his earthly ministry (John 17:14–16). Later on, Peter exhorts believers to make this alien witness real based on Christ's establishment of our peculiar identity (1 Pet. 2:9–12). Believers are pilgrims in this world. While one day this earth will be restored to its Edenic glory, this time incorruptible, the presence of sin and Satan in the meantime must make us ever mindful that "our citizenship is in heaven" (Phil. 3:20).

THE GREAT COMMANDMENT. Paul echoes Leviticus 19:18 and Deuteronomy 6:4–6 in Romans 13:8–9, just as Jesus did in the Great Commandment (Matt. 22:37–39; Mark 12:29–31; Luke 10:27). From beginning to end, the call of the Bible to the people of God is the call to love. We are summoned to serve God with gladness as his redeemed people and to serve others with childlike, self-divesting delight. This is our only true joy. It is what it means to be human.

Theological Soundings

SPIRITUAL WORSHIP. We are used to thinking of worship as something we do in a church gathering, primarily through singing songs. This is an important aspect of worship, but real worship is much broader and deeper than mere singing. Paul gets at the fuller dimension of worship in Romans 12:1, when he appeals to his readers to present their very bodies in an act of worship. He calls them to become living sacrifices, which is their "spiritual worship." What does this mean? To be a living sacrifice is to live in such a way of openness and availability and abandon to God's will that it reflects how much we are trusting the loving sacrifice of Jesus. This is why Paul says we do this "by the mercies of God." Because the Spirit isn't simply sitting in a church building, waiting for us to come visit him in worship of God, but has occupied our bodies, our bodies may worship at many more moments than in church worship services. So spiritual worship is all-encompassing. And because we are able to worship "by God's mercies," our worship is not man-generated, but Spirit-generated.

SPIRITUAL GIFTS. In Romans 12:3–8, Paul touches on some of the ways in which the Holy Spirit gifts us in God's grace for ministry to each other in the building up of the church. Paul's primary points in this passage are that what God establishes in life he will equip for growth and that as people of all tongues, tribes, and nations are united in Christ, we have the spiritual tools we need to live in Christ-centered harmony and power. Everyone plays a part, and nobody is the hero or star of the church except Jesus himself. We are all in service to him.

CHURCH AND STATE. Here is an interesting implication of gospel freedom: submission to governmental authorities. In Romans 13:1–7 Paul commands Christians to respect and pray for the civil authorities in their land. We should never become cowardly or sinfully compromising about what God explicitly tells us not to do, of course, but that is not what Paul is urging. Rather, he is charging us to trust God with our hearts and souls, to put our hope in Christ, not in any governmental program or authority. This applies equally to our resentments or grievances with the government. If we are not being induced to sin by the law of our land, we are tasked with being "in subjection" (13:5), to pay what is owed (13:7), and to respect and honor authorities (13:7). This is very hard to do in contemporary political climates, but it was just as hard to do in Paul's day, especially as the Roman government increasingly persecuted Jesus' church throughout the first two centuries of the church's existence. The witness of the early church regarding governmental authorities is instructive and enlightening. It is a great cross-centered challenge to the church today.

Personal Implications

Take time to reflect on the implications of Romans 12:1–13:14 for your own life today. Make notes below on the personal implications for your walk with the Lord of (1) the *Gospel Glimpses*, (2) the *Whole-Bible Connections*, (3) the *Theological Soundings*, and (4) this passage as a whole.

1. Gospel Glimpses

----

2. Whole-Bible Connections

3. Theological Soundings

4. Romans 12:1–13:14

> ### As You Finish This Unit . . .

Take a moment to ask for the Lord's blessing and help as you continue in this study of Romans. And take a moment also to look back through this unit of study, to reflect on some key things that the Lord may be teaching you.

Definitions

[1] **Sacrifice** – An offering to God, often to signify forgiveness of sin. The law of Moses gave detailed instructions regarding various kinds of sacrifices. By his death on the cross, Jesus gave himself as a sacrifice to atone for the sins of believers (Eph. 5:2; Heb. 10:12). Believers are to offer their bodies as living sacrifices to God (Rom. 12:1).

[2] **Reconciliation** – The restoration of an affirmative relationship and peace between alienated or opposing parties. Through his death and resurrection, Jesus has reconciled believers to God (2 Cor. 5:18–21).

WEEK 11:
THE EXTENSION OF
GOD'S RIGHTEOUSNESS
THROUGH MISSION

Romans 14:1–16:23

From beginning to end in the Bible we see that our God is a missionary God. Everyone falls short of his glory (Rom. 3:23), so he wants the message of his righteousness revealed in his Son, Jesus Christ, to go out to everyone. Even in selecting one nation among many—Israel—his plan was that this nation would further the mission of taking the gospel to all nations (Acts 13:47; Rom. 11:11–12). This purpose underlies Paul's letter to the Romans all along, and in Romans 14:1–16:23 this implicit goal becomes explicit. The reason God has allowed the partial and temporary hardening for Israel is to prosper God's saving mission toward the Gentiles. Paul begins the passage by continuing the instructions on interpersonal relationships, for even this is an aspect of mission. The church living in loving unity is a witness to the unbelieving world, and Jews and Greeks reconciled in the gospel is a powerful testimony to the uniting power of grace. From this interpersonal witness, then, Paul goes on through Romans 15 to discuss his particular missionary work as a Jew to Gentiles.

The Big Picture

Romans 14:1–16:23 is concerned with the motives and means of gospel mission in Paul's life and ministry.

Reflection and Discussion

Read through the complete passage for this study, Romans 14:1–16:23. Then review the shorter passages below and write your own notes on the following questions. (For further background, see the *ESV Study Bible*, pages 2180–2185; also available online at esv.org.)

1. Interpersonal Reconciliation (14:1–15:13)

How is reconciliation between believers a good witness?

What are some modern examples that would be our equivalent to the questions concerning "diet" and "days" (14:1–7)?

According to Romans 14:7–8, what is the guiding principle in navigating these issues? How can these issues cause stumbling?

How would you summarize Romans 14:1–15:7 in a single sentence?

2. The Establishment of Churches among the Gentiles (15:14–33)

What is the common denominator in all of the Old Testament texts Paul cites in 15:9–12? What point is he driving home?

In 15:15 Paul says he has been "bold" with the Romans, and in 15:17 he says he has pride in his work. Is Paul sinning in such boldness and pride? What distinctions need to be made between "good boldness" and "bad boldness," good pride and bad pride?

In 1 Corinthians 3:6 Paul says, "I planted, Apollos watered, but God gave the growth" (see also v. 10). Compare this passage in 1 Corinthians to what Paul says in Romans 15:20–24. Taking these two texts together, how would you describe Paul's driving passion?

3. Appreciation and Greetings to Coworkers in the Gospel (16:1–23)

What do we learn about Paul and his ministry from the greetings he gives in Romans 16:1–16? Note that he says something specific about almost every person he mentions.

Read Matthew 10:16. Note what Paul says in Romans 16:19. Unpack the paradox embedded in such texts for the way Christians are to lead their lives.

In Romans 16:20, Paul says that the God of peace will crush Satan[1] under our feet. What is significant about the way he expresses this truth? Consider Genesis 3:15 in your answer.

Read through the following three sections on *Gospel Glimpses, Whole-Bible Connections,* and *Theological Soundings.* Then take time to reflect on the *Personal Implications* these sections have for your walk with the Lord.

Gospel Glimpses

EVERYTHING IS CLEAN. The new covenant has dawned. God's people are no longer instructed to eat only certain foods and to observe in a ceremonial way certain days. For this reason, as Paul says in Romans 14:20, "everything is . . . clean." Yet the same grace that has washed over the world in Jesus and cleansed all of life for believers is the grace that impels believers to act in love for one another. If a brother or sister has a scrupulous conscience, we are to set aside our own free conscience for the sake of that person. The gospel frees us. And the gospel binds us. As Martin Luther wrote concerning Christian liberty, "The Christian is the most free lord of all, subject to none; and the Christian is the most dutiful servant of all, subject to everyone."

GRACE BE WITH YOU. Paul generally opens his letters with "Grace to you" (e.g., Rom. 1:7). And he generally closes with "Grace with you." In Romans, we find him closing the letter this way: "The grace of our Lord Jesus Christ be with you" (16:20). As Paul has taught us in this very letter, faith comes from hearing (10:17), so he knows that the word of God has the spiritual power in it to open the right ears to hear it. This is what is behind Paul's greetings and closings. He wants his readers to know the grace of God, and so he has embedded a prayer in his address. When he writes the biblical letters, because they are not only written by him but also, more broadly, written by God through him, grace is coming *to* hearers/readers. And when the letter is done, grace is now *with* hearers/readers.

Whole-Bible Connections

VINDICATION. "The God of peace will soon crush Satan under your feet," Paul assures the church in Romans 16:20. There are a few interesting things about this short verse, but one of them is its promised fulfillment of something forecast as early as Genesis 3:14–15: "The LORD God said to the serpent . . . 'I will put enmity between you and the woman, and between your offspring and her offspring; he shall bruise your head, and you shall bruise his heel.'" Some theologians call this the *proto-evangelium* (or "first gospel"), because it prophesies the dynamic at the cross, wherein Jesus dies but through his death and resurrection triumphs over sin and Satan (Col. 2:13–15). At the cross, God crushes sin by crushing his Son (Isaiah 53:10), and in this way crushing Satan for us. Consequently, we who are at peace with God carry the power of the cross to crush Satan as well. God's righteousness is vindicated—or proved—at the cross, and so is his possession of us. Paul celebrates this in Romans 16:20 and issues it as a hope and promise, as well as a missional activity!

REJOICE, O GENTILES! Paul strings together several Old Testament texts in Romans 15:9–12 to demonstrate the truth that Christ came not least "in order that the Gentiles might glorify God for his mercy" (15:9). All through the Bible, the careful reader will discern God's strange inversions—extending mercy to those whom one would least expect, while those who ought to be recipients of God's mercy wind up excluded. The greatest instance of this is the inclusion of the Gentiles. And Paul says not only that the Gentiles will be saved but that they will rejoice at this salvation. "Let all the peoples extol him" (15:11). God is glorified preeminently by his people rejoicing in him. And one day a "ransomed people for God from every tribe and language and people and nation" will extol him together in the new earth (Rev. 5:9).

Theological Soundings

CHRISTIAN LIBERTY. Romans 14 covers a subject known as Christian liberty. Because Christians are set free from the law of ordinances (Eph. 2:15) and are under grace (Rom. 6:14), we are free to follow our Spirit-informed consciences[2] in matters on which the Bible is silent. In Paul's day, the primary issues facing the church in the uneasy mix of Jews and Gentiles was eating meat sacrificed to idols (1 Cor. 10:23–33). As this section of Romans demonstrates, the questions of an omnivorous or herbivorous diet have arisen once more, along with the honoring of certain days for ceremonial reasons. Paul commends the Christian to his conscience on these matters, but transcending even that freedom, he wants Christ to be honored and our neighbors to be loved. So while we are free to do that which is not sin, we are not free to exercise liberty in a way that does not edify or serve our brothers and sisters. Paul's admonishment thus cuts both ways: stronger brothers should not parade their liberty, while weaker brothers should not judge the stronger.

MISSIO DEI. Romans 14–16 exemplifies a biblical doctrine theologians often call the *Missio Dei*, which means "the mission of God." God is drawing a people to himself, for his own possession and for his own glory. It is for this reason that he calls Abraham and Moses, that he sends the prophets, and climactically, that he sends his Son, and then the Holy Spirit. God is a sending God, and we are a sent people. The ultimate goal of this mission is not only to call people to himself, but to restore the entire created order (Rom. 8:19–22). The whole universe will one day work as it was meant to.

JUDGMENT ACCORDING TO WORKS. The Bible teaches that believers are fully and finally acquitted (justified) on the basis of Christ's finished work, received through faith. Yet the Bible also teaches that believers will be judged according to their works, to receive such rewards as their discipleship warrants. One example of this is Romans 14:10–12 (see also 1 Cor. 3:10–15; 2 Cor. 5:10; Gal. 6:7–9). It is difficult to reconcile these two teachings, yet we must submit to Scripture at every point and seek to bring our minds under its authority. While on the one hand believers can rest assured that their justification is a settled matter (Rom. 5:1), we must also be sobered by the fact that a life devoid of any spiritual fruit gives reason to doubt that such a person has indeed been justified. For everyone who has been justified—and also, therefore, united to Christ and indwelt by the Spirit—will necessarily live in a different, more godly way than before. As the reformer John Calvin said, "It is faith alone that justifies, but the faith that justifies is never alone." Godliness is the evidence of faith.

Personal Implications

Take time to reflect on the implications of Romans 14:1–16:23 for your own life today. Make notes below on the personal implications for your walk with the Lord of (1) the *Gospel Glimpses*, (2) the *Whole-Bible Connections*, (3) the *Theological Soundings*, and (4) this passage as a whole.

1. Gospel Glimpses

2. Whole-Bible Connections

3. Theological Soundings

4. Romans 14:1–16:23

> ## As You Finish This Unit . . .

Take a moment to ask for the Lord's blessing and help as you continue in this study of Romans. And take a moment also to look back through this unit of study, to reflect on some key things that the Lord may be teaching you.

Definitions

[1] **Satan** – A spiritual being whose name means "accuser." As the leader of all the demonic forces, he opposes God's rule and seeks to harm God's people and accuse them of wrongdoing. His power, however, is confined to the bounds that God has set for him, and one day he will be destroyed along with all his demons (Matt. 25:41; Rev. 20:10).

[2] **Conscience** – The ability to understand tacitly the rightness or wrongness of one's actions and motives. The conscience is not identical with the inner witness of the Holy Spirit, although the Holy Spirit often employs the conscience in guiding people and convicting them of sin (Rom. 2:15).

WEEK 12:
FINAL SUMMARY OF
THE GOSPEL OF THE
RIGHTEOUSNESS OF GOD

Romans 16:25–27

▲

All along Paul has been exulting. That is to say, all along he has been worshiping as he is writing. Paul has been so captured by God's grace that he cannot instruct without celebrating, rebuke without grieving, and command without assuring. He is so utterly convinced of God's deep love in the grace of Jesus Christ that worship regularly erupts from his heart. He wants it to erupt in our hearts too; that is the point of his writing in the first place. As he gets to the end of his letter to the Roman church, then, he bursts out one final time in praise of God. This short prayer encapsulates the main themes of what he has written. And he does all this as an act of unabashed praise.

What is the ultimate point of Paul's letter to the Romans? The same as the Bible's ultimate point: that God's glory through Jesus Christ would be magnified everywhere at every time.

The Big Picture

Romans 16:25–27 is a doxology[1] in which Paul gathers up in a few brief lines, as a final song of praise to God, all that he has said in his letter to the Romans.

Reflection and Discussion

Read through the complete passage for this study, Romans 16:25–27. Then write your own notes on the following questions. (For further background, see the *ESV Study Bible*, page 2185; also available online at esv.org.)

What themes crop up in Romans 16:25–27 that also appeared in 1:1–7?

In what specific areas of your life do you most need gospel strength right now (16:25)?

What does Paul mean when he calls the gospel message a "mystery" (16:25)? As you answer, consider Ephesians 3:3–6; 6:19; Colossians 1:26–27.

Paul says that the gospel is not only a mystery that has been revealed but also a prophecy that has been fulfilled. What Old Testament prophecies can you think of that point to Christ?

How is God's glory—the full "weight" of all his attributes, characteristics, and self-ness—revealed through Jesus Christ?

As you reflect on your study through Paul's letter to the Romans, what are some things that stand out to you? What are the major things you have learned?

What are some parts of this study that have challenged you? How are you different after studying Romans?

Read through the following three sections on *Gospel Glimpses, Whole-Bible Connections,* and *Theological Soundings.* Then take time to reflect on the *Personal Implications* these sections have for your walk with the Lord.

Gospel Glimpses

GOSPEL STRENGTH. Paul prays for his readers in Romans 16:25–27, claiming that God is able to strengthen them "according to my gospel and the preaching of Jesus Christ" (16:25). Part of the good news is that the good news gives us strength. The gospel creates its own implications. As Paul had said at the beginning of the letter, the gospel is "power" (Rom. 1:16). The gospel of grace not only ignites the Christian life but sustains it. As Paul says in another letter, the gospel is that "in which you stand, and by which you are being saved" (1 Cor. 15:1–2).

"THE OBEDIENCE OF FAITH." All who exercise faith will necessarily produce a fruitful life of obedience. Faith and obedience must be kept strictly separate regarding justification, but they must be kept closely together regarding Christian living. Obedience flows from faith. As we trust in the Lord and enjoy our gracious status as his children, our hearts are transformed from the inside out. Our behavior changes. Fruit is borne. Such fruit is not what saves us; faith, uniting us to Christ, does. We are not saved *by* obedience, but neither are we saved *without* it.

Whole-Bible Connections

THE MYSTERY OF CHRIST. This concluding doxology also takes us back to revisit the reality that Christ is the full-light arrival of what lay in the shadows of the old covenant (Heb. 10:1). In another part of the New Testament, Peter highlights the same searching secret (1 Pet. 1:10–12). Peter says Jesus is the promise "now announced." Paul says Jesus is the promise "now disclosed" (Rom. 16:26). From such passages we learn that the revelation of the Old Testament displayed the glory of Christ throughout its pages, from the covering given to Adam and Eve at the beginning of the Old Testament (Gen. 3:21) to the covering given to Joshua the priest at the end of the Old Testament (Zech. 3:1–5). The entire Old Testament longs for someone to come and fulfill all the promises God had made to his people. Jesus Christ is that man. Paul says that the gospel mystery was made known "through the prophetic writings" (Rom. 16:26). The New Testament does not move off in a different direction; the New Testament fulfills and completes the revelation given and begun in the Old Testament.

Theological Soundings

GOD'S ETERNALITY. Paul speaks of "the command of the eternal God" in Romans 16:26. God is eternal. In terms of time, he never had a beginning and he will never have an end. He simply *is*. As God revealed to Moses, he is simply

"I AM" (Ex. 3:14). Our human lives are trapped in time, and we cannot manipulate time to pass any more slowly or quickly. God, however, transcends time itself. He *created* time.

GOD'S GLORY. The final words in Romans read, "to the only wise God be glory forevermore through Jesus Christ! Amen"² (16:27). To define God's "glory" is difficult because from one perspective his glory is simply who he is, in all that he is. The full range of his attributes together make God glorious. God's glory is his resplendence, his holy beauty, his utterly supreme magnificence.

Personal Implications

Take time to reflect on the implications of Romans 16:25–27 for your own life today. Make notes below on the personal implications for your walk with the Lord of (1) the *Gospel Glimpses*, (2) the *Whole-Bible Connections*, (3) the *Theological Soundings*, and (4) this passage as a whole.

1. Gospel Glimpses

2. Whole-Bible Connections

3. Theological Soundings

4. Romans 16:25–27

▶ As You Finish This Unit . . .

Take a moment to ask for the Lord's blessing and help as you continue in this study of Romans. And take a moment also to look back through this unit of study, to reflect on some key things that the Lord may be teaching you.

▶ As You Finish Studying Romans . . .

We rejoice with you as you finish studying the book of Romans! May this study become part of your Christian walk of faith, day by day and week by week throughout all your life. Now we would greatly encourage you to study the Word of God on a week-by-week basis. To continue your study of the Bible, we would encourage you to consider other books in the *Knowing the Bible* series, and to visit www.knowingthebibleseries.org.

Lastly, take a moment to look back through this study. Review the notes that you have written, and the things that you have highlighted or underlined. Reflect again on the key themes that the Lord has been teaching you about himself and about his Word. May these things become a treasure for you throughout your life—which we pray will be true for you, in the name of the Father, and the Son, and the Holy Spirit. Amen.

Definitions

[1] **Doxology** – Expression of praise to God. Often included at the end of New Testament letters. Modern church services often end with doxologies in the form of short hymns.

[2] **Amen** – Greek form of a Hebrew word meaning "to confirm." In Scripture and in Christian life, when uttered after a prayer or statement, it means "let it be so."